THE BOOK OF

PRESERVES

JAMS · CHUTNEYS · PICKLES · JELLIES

T H E   B O O K   O F
PRESERVES
JAMS · CHUTNEYS · PICKLES · JELLIES

MARY NORWAK

Photography by JON STEWART

HPBooks®

ANOTHER BEST SELLING VOLUME FROM HP BOOKS®

Published by HP Books®, P.O. Box 5367, Tucson, AZ 85703   602/888–2150
ISBN: 0–89586–507–6
Library of Congress Card Number: 86–81351
1st Printing

By arrangement with Salamander Books Limited and
Merehurst Press, London

NOTICE: The information contained in this book is true and complete to the best
of our knowledge. All recommendations are made without any guarantees on the
part of the author or HP Books®. The author and publisher disclaim all liability
in connection with the use of this information.

Publisher: Rick Bailey
Editorial Director: Elaine Woodard
Editors: Patricia Aaron, Hilary Walden, Chris Fayers
Designers: Roger Daniels, Richard Slater, Stuart Willard
Food stylist: Barbara Stewart
Photographer: Jon Stewart
Typeset by Lineage
Color separation and printing by New Interlitho S.p.A., Milan

Contents

INTRODUCTION

Preserving is one of the oldest and most satisfying forms of cooking. For hundreds of years, cooks have enjoyed preparing their bounty of summer fruit and vegetables in a variety of ways in order to prepare delicious meals during the less plentiful days of winter.

Until partway through the 20th century, a country household aimed to be totally self-sufficient, drying fruit, vegetables and herbs, preparing pickles, chutneys and sauces and making jams and other delicious sweet preserves. Candying fruit, making liqueurs or bottling fruit in alcohol were activities of more leisured wives who could afford time and a little extra money for preserving their fruits.

Today, freezers deal with bulky supplies, but preserving is such a satisfying activity that many people enjoy it as a leisure pastime. Additionally, there is now a strong feeling for old-fashioned ways of past years and for the nostalgic delicacies which so delighted our ancestors. While families obviously enjoy results, cooks get great pleasure from offering specialities as gifts. Presentation is almost as important as initial preparation.

In this book, recipes are provided for unusual preserves which are not difficult to prepare, will give a special touch to everyday meals and will make delightful and welcome presents for all occasions.

UTENSILS

Equipment for preserving is not expensive or difficult to obtain. Many items are already in household use. It is important to use correct utensils to ensure good results.

Large, heavy-based saucepan or preserving pan is essential so preserves containing sugar do not burn. A pan should be large so jam may be boiled hard without boiling over and wide enough to allow rapid evaporation of liquid to aid setting. A true preserving pan does not have a long handle, which could be dangerous, but is fitted with a pair of short looped handles, or a bail (a carrying handle over the top). A suitable saucepan may be used if necessary. A pan should be made of aluminium or stainless steel. Copper will help to keep green fruits green, but will spoil the color of red fruit. Chipped enamel can be dangerous, while zinc or iron can spoil color or flavor.

Long handled wooden spoon is necessary as preserves are very hot and hands should be well away from danger of splashing.

Strainer or sieve is useful when preparing purées. It should have a non-metallic mesh to prevent discoloration.

Kitchen scales or measuring jugs are needed, as correct proportions of ingredients are necessary for success. Careful weighing or measuring is important.

Large mixing bowl is needed, particularly for preparing pickles and chutneys. Choose one made of ovenglass, earthenware or stainless steel.

Candy thermometer is useful to check setting point of preserves, jams and jellies.

Jam funnel is a small inexpensive item which is useful for helping to keep jars clean when filling.

Jelly bag is necessary for preparing jellies and syrups. It is suspended from its own stand. If not available, a piece of cheesecloth may be used instead.

Stainless steel slotted spoon is useful for removing foam from jams and jellies, and also lifting and draining solid ingredients which must be packed into jars.

Jars may be new or used and should be scrupulously clean. Screwtop or clip jars are useful for many preserves. Lids need vinegar-proof linings for pickles, chutneys and sauces.

Jars for herbs should be small and made of dark glass to prevent penetration of light and fading of contents.

INGREDIENTS

Fruit

Choose fresh and firm, not mushy fruit. It should be slightly under-ripe. Very ripe fruit has reduced sugar content which will affect setting and quality. Sort fruit carefully and discard any bruised or damaged pieces. If fruit needs to be washed, with the exception of berries, place in a sieve or colander under cold running water and carefully dry. Wash fruit low in pectin, such as strawberries, as little as possible. Pit or peel fruit with stainless steel or silver kitchen tools to prevent discoloration. Prepare fruit immediately before cooking or fruit will deteriorate.

Vegetables

For pickles and chutneys, vegetables should be ready for eating. Do not choose over-mature vegetables or they become tough and stringy. Wash well and dry, then peel or otherwise prepare as necessary. As with fruit, prepare immediately before use.

Dried Fruit

All dried fruit should be plump, fresh and of high quality. If washing is necessary, place fruit in a sieve or colander and rinse under cold running water. Dry completely before using.

Sugar

Granulated sugar may be used for all preserves. Brown sugars are often used to give color and flavor to pickles, chutneys and sauces. They do not give a good set to sweet preserves, although the flavor is delicious. Honey also gives a good flavor but prevents firm setting.

Dissolve sugar slowly and carefully in preserves by heating gently and stirring occasionally. If sugar crystals remain undissolved, they may burn on the bottom of the pan, and affect smoothness of finished product. Warm sugar slightly in a warm oven before adding to fruit, and it will dissolve more quickly.

Vinegar

Use vinegar of good quality and containing at least 5% acetic acid or it will not preserve fruit or vegetables. Malt vinegar has a strong flavor and color. White vinegar is preferable for clear pickles and spiced fruit although the flavor is very strong. Wine vinegar and cider vinegar give a better flavor to more delicate preserves. Ready-spiced vinegar may be purchased. More individual flavors can be achieved by using whole spices infused in warm vinegar.

Acid

Lemon juice, citric or tartaric acid are added to some fruits before cooking to extract pectin, improve color and prevent crystallization. To 4 pounds fruit, allow 2 tablespoons lemon juice or ½ teaspoon citric or tartaric acid.

Pectin

The pectin content of fruit affects setting quality of jams and jellies. Fruits with *High Pectin Content* include apples, blackcurrants, damsons, gooseberries, plums and redcurrants. *Medium Pectin Content* fruits include apricots, early blackberries, greengages and loganberries. *Low Pectin Content* fruits include late blackberries, cherries, pears, rhubarb, raspberries, strawberries and tomatoes. Seeds and pith of fruit contain pectin and are sometimes cooked with fruit. Pectin may be introduced into a preserve with a mixture of fruit, such as apples with blackberries. Commercial pectin may be added to preserves. Follow manufacturers' instructions carefully.

Spices

Use fresh and fragrant spices or a musty flavor will develop. Whole spices are usually tied into a cheesecloth bag and suspended in pan during preparation and then discarded. A few whole spices may be included in some preserves to give a stronger flavor during maturation and to give an attractive appearance.

SETTING, PACKING AND SEALING PRESERVES

Setting Tests

A preserve for storage needs 60% added sugar content, or 3 parts sugar to 5 parts preserve. Some preserves are ready for setting after boiling rapidly 5 minutes while others need to boil rapidly 20 minutes. Make setting tests at 5 minute intervals. If a preserve is boiled too long, it will never set. When preserve reaches setting point, remove from heat at once. There are three setting tests:

a) **Temperature test** – dip a candy thermometer in hot water. Stir preserve and submerge the thermometer bulb in preserve. When thermometer registers 221F (105C), the preserve is ready.

b) **Plate test** – remove pan from heat and pour a small amount of preserve on a cold plate. Let stand until cold. If preserve forms a skin and wrinkles when pushed with a finger, it is ready.

c) **Sheeting test** – dip a chilled spoon in the boiling preserve. Let preserve drip from the spoon. When preserve no longer falls off spoon in drips, but in a sheet, preserve is ready.

Packing

Wash jars in hot soapy water; rinse. After washing, plunge jars into boiling water. Dry on side of a hot range or in a warm oven. When preserve is ready, remove pan from heat. If preserve contains solid fruit or peel, let stand 5 to 10 minutes. Stir preserve gently so fruit will not rise in jars. Ladle into jars, using a jam funnel fitted into neck of jar. Fill jar to the top (but if sealing with paraffin fill to ⅛-inch of top). Tap jar gently to release air bubbles.

Sealing

Wipe rim of jar with a clean damp cloth. Close canning jars with hot self-sealing vacuum lids. Screw metal band down firmly by hand. If sealing with paraffin, spoon a ⅛-inch layer of melted paraffin over preserve, covering completely. Cool 5 to 10 minutes until paraffin hardens. Place another spoonful of melted paraffin on top. Lift and turn container so paraffin runs ¼-inch or more up side of jar. Cool 24 hours. Cover with lid or foil.

Boiling Water Bath

Canner must be deep enough for closed jars to be covered with boiling water. Place closed jars on rack in bottom of canner leaving enough room between jars for water to circulate. When all jars are in place, pour hot water around jars until water is 1 to 2 inches above jars. Cover canner; bring water to a full boil. Begin counting processing time. Reduce heat until water boils gently. When processing time is finished, remove jars. Set on a wire rack or towels. Let cool 10 to 12 hours.

Pressure-Canner

Follow manufacturer's directions. Correct operation of canner is critical for a safe and appealing preserve.

Storage

When firmly set, store in a cool, dry, dark place.

PACKAGING

Jars or bottles

Choose a container which is suitable for contents. Pickles and chutneys look inviting in professional preserving jars with screwtop or clip-on lids. If made for a gift, they might be packaged in an antique or modern pickle jar ready for a table. Expensive conserves look very special in decorative and unusually shaped jars rather than traditional straight-sided jelly jars. Jellies are often needed in small quantities for one-meal servings, and can be ladled into small jars. Curds can be placed in small bowls.

Vinegars can be bottled in flasks ready for a table, and mustards in jars which can go straight on a condiment tray. Liqueurs can be bottled in traditional bottles. A small quantity for a gift might be decanted into an individual flask.

Cleanliness

While containers have been cleaned and sterilized before use, they can become messy during preparation and filling. While still hot, containers can be wiped with a soft cloth dipped in warm water and detergent, and carefully dried. When contents are cold, polish jars with a cloth dipped in methylated spirit.

Labels

All preserves should be clearly and informatively labeled. Labels should be clean, neat, carefully written, and applied on container.

Covers

All preserves must be firmly and tightly sealed, but tops of jars are not always sightly. Use polished or colored metal or plastic tops without identification. If trade-names are on reused containers, paint with enamel or cover with a circle of stick-on plastic fabric.

A most attractive finishing touch can be made by tying a thin string or decorative tape or ribbon around a paper or cotton fabric topping. For a special effect, cut paper or fabric with pinking shears. Use cheerful bold checked or plain fabric for pickles, chutneys or everyday sweet preserves, and very pretty patterns for conserves, curds or fruit in alcohol.

Presentation Gifts

A collection of preserves or a single jar or bottle can make a very attractive gift, but it is pleasant to give something extra to make a present memorable. Five single jars of jam in a box covered with pretty paper or foil, together with a little jam dish or a spoon, or give a flask of liqueur with a suitable glass or a jar of conserve or fruit in alcohol with a serving bowl or a jar of cream.

If a number of jars are packaged together, try to vary coverings to make a more interesting collection. Again, add a suitable complementary item such as a wedge of cheese with two or three pickles, or a serving tray to hold a variety of preserves.

A strong box neatly covered with pretty wrapping paper or foil makes a good container. Crumpled paper or polythene granules keep glass and bottles safe. Baskets look good, or items such as a new pan, colander or serving tray. Finish the gift with plenty of ribbons and an attractive gift card.

LABELING

Clearly written labels are essential to identify all types of preserves. They may be decorative as well as informative. Labels for each batch of jars or bottles should be identical, so they are easily recognized. Labels should be clean and unwrinkled, and applied neatly on jars. Write in water-proof ink, never in pencil so label remains clear. Some suggestions for making your own labels are shown in the picture below, and add these relevant details:

a) *Name of preserve*
If preserve is traditionally known as something like "Anna's Special Jelly", add main flavoring ingredients.
b) *Date of preparation*
This is final date of packaging, sealing and labeling.
c) *Eat-by date*
In case of short-life preparations such as Lemon Curd, this should be date after which preserve becomes unattractive or inedible. Pickles and chutneys can have a maturity date after which they will be excellent to eat.
d) *Special Notes*
This need only be indicated on unfamiliar preserves, not on basic jams; to tell recipient best ways of using contents.

JAMS

Jam is made of fruits or fruit juices, pectin, acid and sugar. It is less firm than jelly. Fruits, such as apples, plums, lemons, limes and oranges, are high in pectin content, which, when combined with sugar, helps jam to set. Strawberries, cherries and peaches are low in pectin content, and lemon juice is often added to these fruits to aid setting and bring out the flavor of the fruit.

Use sound, slightly under-ripe fruit which is not mushy. Wash and dry. Remove stems, leaves and any bruised parts. Prepare fruit according to recipe.

In a large saucepan, simmer fruit and water until fruit is soft and mixture is reduced by ½.

Add sugar. Stir until sugar dissolves.

Increase heat. Bring to a boil. Boil rapidly until jam reaches 221F (105C).

Remove from heat. Test for setting. Cool a small amount of jam on a cool plate 1 minute. Push with a finger to form wrinkles.

Skim jam to remove foam. Cool 5 to 10 minutes. Stir well. Ladle hot jam into hot jars; cover and label. Process in a boiling water bath, page 13, following recipe directions.

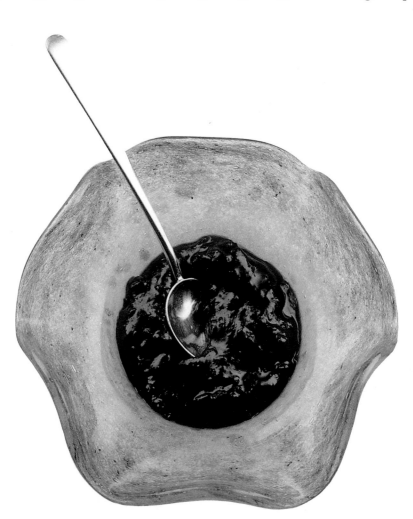

Plum and Cherry Brandy Jam

3 lb. plums, pitted, coarsely chopped

⅔ cup water

8 tablespoons lemon juice

7 cups sugar

4 tablespoons cherry brandy

Wash 12 (½ pint) jars in hot soapy water; rinse. Keep hot until needed. Prepare lids as manufacturer directs.

In a large saucepan, cook plums and water over low heat until plums are very soft. Add lemon juice. Simmer 5 minutes. Add sugar. Stir until sugar dissolves. Increase heat; boil rapidly for 15 minutes or until jam reaches 221F (105C).

Remove from heat. Stir in cherry brandy. Skim off foam. Let stand 5 minutes.

Stir well. Ladle hot jam into 1 hot jar at a time. Wipe rim of jar with a clean damp cloth. Attach lid. Fill and close remaining jars. Place in canner.

Process in a boiling water bath, page 13, 10 minutes.

Makes 12 (½ pints).

Peach and Raspberry Jam

2 lb. peaches, peeled, sliced

⅔ cup water

2 tablespoons lemon juice

6⅓ cups raspberries, stems removed

6 cups sugar

Wash 10 (½ pint) jars in hot soapy water; rinse. Keep hot until needed. Prepare lids as manufacturer directs.

In a large saucepan, simmer peaches, water and lemon juice until peaches are soft. Add raspberries. Simmer 5 minutes. Add sugar. Stir until sugar dissolves. Increase heat; boil rapidly 15 to 20 minutes until jam reaches 221F (105C). Remove from heat. Skim off foam. Cool 5 to 10 minutes.

Ladle hot jam into 1 hot jar at a time. Wipe rim of jar with a clean damp cloth. Attach lid. Fill and close remaining jars. Place in canner.

Process in a boiling water bath, page 13, 10 minutes.

Makes 10 (½ pints).

Rhubarb and Angelica Jam

4 lb. rhubarb, cut in 1-inch pieces

6 cups sugar

½ teaspoon citric acid

1 cup chopped crystallized angelica

In a large bowl, alternate layers of rhubarb and sugar. Let stand in a cool place 24 hours.

Wash 10 (½ pint) jars in hot soapy water; rinse. Keep hot until needed. Prepare lids as manufacturer directs.

In a large saucepan, bring rhubarb, sugar and citric acid to a boil, stirring continuously. Reduce heat; simmer 10 minutes. Increase heat; boil rapidly 10 minutes or until jam reaches 221F (105C).

Remove from heat. Stir in angelica. Skim off foam. Let stand 5 minutes.

Stir well. Ladle hot jam into 1 hot jar at a time. Wipe rim of jar with a clean damp cloth. Attach lid. Fill and close remaining jars. Place in canner.

Process in a boiling water bath, page 13, 10 minutes.

Makes 10 (½ pints).

Pear and Peach Jam

2 lb. ripe pears

1½ lb. peaches, peeled, sliced, pitted

⅔ cup water

6 cups sugar

Grated peel and juice of 3 lemons

Wash 10 (½ pint) jars in hot soapy water; rinse. Keep hot until needed. Prepare lids as manufacturer directs.

Peel and core pears; tie cores in a cheesecloth bag. Chop flesh.

In a large saucepan bring pears, cheesecloth bag, peaches and water to a boil. Reduce heat; simmer until fruit is soft. Add sugar, lemon peel and juice. Stir until sugar dissolves. Increase heat; boil rapidly 15 to 20 minutes or until jam reaches 221F (105C). Remove from heat. Skim off foam. Cool 5 to 10 minutes.

Ladle hot jam into 1 hot jar at a time. Wipe rim of jar with a clean damp cloth. Attach lid. Fill and close remaining jars. Place in canner.

Process in a boiling water bath, page 13, 10 minutes.

Makes 10 (½ pints).

Apricot and Date Low Sugar Jam

3 cups dried apricots

5 cups water

4½ cups pitted dates, chopped

1 cup sugar

Juice of 1 lemon

½ cup almonds, chopped

In a large bowl combine apricots and ½ of water. Let stand 12 hours.

Wash 5 (½ pint) jars in hot soapy water; rinse. Keep hot until needed. Prepare lids as manufacturer directs.

In a large saucepan, simmer apricots and liquid, remaining water and dates until apricots are soft. Add sugar and lemon juice. Stir until sugar dissolves. Simmer until jam thickens; stir in almonds. Cook 2 minutes. Remove from heat. Skim off foam. Cool 5 to 10 minutes.

Ladle hot jam into 1 hot jar at a time. Wipe rim of jar with a clean damp cloth. Attach lid. Fill and close remaining jars. Place in canner.

Process in a boiling water bath, page 13, 10 minutes.

Makes 5 (½ pints).

Apple Ginger Jam

3 lb. tart apples, peeled, cored, thinly sliced

2½ cups water

Grated peel and juice of 2 lemons

1 teaspoon ground ginger

6 cups sugar

½ cup chopped crystallized ginger

Wash 10 (½ pint) jars in hot soapy water; rinse. Keep hot until needed. Prepare lids as manufacturer directs.

In a large saucepan, simmer apples, water, lemon peel and juice and ground ginger until apples are soft. Add sugar. Stir until sugar dissolves. Increase heat; boil rapidly 15 to 20 minutes or until jam reaches 221F (105C). Remove from heat. Stir in crystallized ginger. Skim off foam. Let stand for 5 to 10 minutes.

Ladle hot jam into 1 hot jar at a time. Wipe rim of jar with a clean damp cloth. Attach lid. Fill and close remaining jars. Place in canner. Process in a boiling water bath, page 13, 10 minutes.

Makes 10 (½ pints).

Fruit Salad Jam

3 cups dried fruit salad (apples, pears, apricots, prunes) coarsely chopped

7½ cups water

3 tablespoons lemon juice

6 cups sugar

In a large bowl, combine fruit salad and water. Let stand 24 hours.

Wash 10 (½ pint) jars in hot soapy water; rinse. Keep hot until needed. Prepare lids as manufacturer directs.

In a large saucepan, simmer fruit salad and liquid 40 minutes. Add lemon juice and sugar. Stir until sugar dissolves. Increase heat; boil rapidly 15 to 20 minutes or until jam reaches 221F (105C).

Remove from heat. Skim off foam. Let stand 5 minutes.

Ladle hot jam into 1 hot jar at a time. Wipe rim of jar with a clean damp cloth. Attach lid. Fill and close remaining jars. Place in canner.

Process in a boiling water bath, page 13, 10 minutes.

Makes 10 (½ pints).

Strawberry Jam

3½ lb. strawberries, hulled

3 tablespoons lemon juice

6 cups sugar

Wash 10 (½ pint) jars in hot soapy water; rinse. Keep hot until needed. Prepare lids as manufacturer directs.

In a large saucepan, simmer strawberries and lemon juice 30 minutes or until strawberries are soft. Add sugar. Stir until sugar dissolves. Increase heat; boil rapidly 15 to 20 minutes or until jam reaches 221F (105C).

Remove from heat. Skim off foam. Let stand 15 minutes.

Stir well. Ladle hot jam into 1 hot jar at a time. Wipe rim of jar with a clean damp cloth. Attach lid. Fill and close remaining jars. Place in canner.

Process in a boiling water bath, page 13, 10 minutes.

Makes 10 (½ pints).

Rose Petal Jam

1 lb. dark red rose petals

3 cups sugar

1¼ cups water

1 tablespoon lemon juice

3 tablespoons rosewater

Snip white bottoms from rose petals; discard. Chop petals coarsely.
In a large bowl, combine chopped petals and ½ of sugar. Let stand,
covered, 48 hours.

Wash 3 (½ pint) jars in hot soapy water; rinse. Keep hot until
needed. Prepare lids as manufacturer directs.

In a large saucepan, cook water, lemon juice and remaining sugar
over low heat until sugar dissolves, stirring continuously. Add rose
petals and liquid. Increase heat; boil rapidly 20 minutes.

Remove from heat. Stir in rosewater. Skim off foam. Let stand 5 to
10 minutes.

Ladle hot jam into 1 hot jar at a time. Wipe rim of jar with a clean
damp cloth. Attach lid. Fill and close remaining jars. Place in canner.

Process in a boiling water bath, page 13, 10 minutes.

Jam has a thick syrup consistency.

Makes 3 (½ pints).

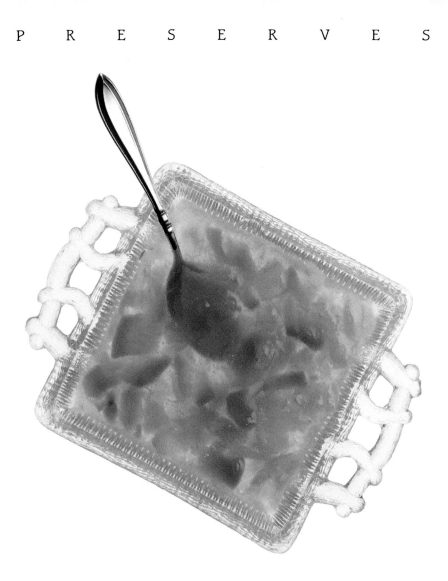

Dried Apricot and Pear Jam

3 cups dried apricots

2½ cups water

3 lb. ripe pears, peeled, coarsely chopped

4 tablespoons lemon juice

7 cups sugar

**3 tablespoons apricot brandy, Grand Marnier
or Curaçao, if desired**

In a large bowl combine apricots and water. Let stand 12 hours.

Wash 12 (½ pint) jars in hot soapy water; rinse. Keep hot until needed. Prepare lids as manufacturer directs.

In a large saucepan, simmer apricots, liquid, pears and lemon juice 20 minutes. Add sugar. Stir until sugar dissolves. Increase heat; boil rapidly 15 to 20 minutes until jam reaches 221F (105C).

Remove from heat. Stir in apricot brandy, Grand Marnier or Curaçao, if desired. Skim off foam. Let stand 5 to 10 minutes.

Ladle hot jam into 1 hot jar at a time. Wipe rim of jar with a clean damp cloth. Attach lid. Fill and close remaining jars. Place in canner. Process in a boiling water bath, page 13, 10 minutes.

Makes 12 (½ pints).

Black Cherry Jam

4 lb. black cherries, pitted

1 teaspoon citric acid

7 cups sugar

Wash 12 (½ pint) jars in hot soapy water; rinse. Keep hot until needed. Prepare lids as manufacturer directs.

In a large saucepan, cook cherries and citric acid over low heat until cherries are very soft. Stir often. Add sugar. Stir until sugar dissolves. Increase heat; boil rapidly 20 minutes or until jam reaches 221F (105C). Remove from heat. Skim off foam. Cool 5 to 10 minutes.

Ladle hot jam into 1 hot jar at a time. Wipe rim of jar with a clean damp cloth. Attach lid. Fill and close remaining jars. Place in canner.

Process in a boiling water bath, page 13, 10 minutes.

Makes 12 (½ pints).

Kiwifruit Jam

2 lb. kiwifruit, peeled, chopped

½ teaspoon citric acid

3 cups sugar

Wash 3 (½ pint) jars in hot soapy water; rinse. Keep hot until needed. Prepare lids as manufacturer directs.

In a large saucepan, cook kiwifruit and citric acid over low heat until kiwifruit is soft. Add sugar. Stir until sugar dissolves. Increase heat, boil rapidly 10 minutes or until jam reaches 221F (105C). Remove from heat. Skim off foam. Cool 5 to 10 minutes.

Ladle hot jam into 1 hot jar at a time. Wipe rim of jar with a clean damp cloth. Attach lid. Fill and close remaining jars. Place in canner.

Process in a boiling water bath, page 13, 10 minutes.

Makes 3 (½ pints).

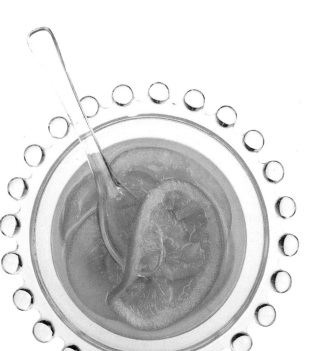

Orange Jam

3 lb. Valencia oranges, thinly sliced

Pinch of salt

3 cups sugar

7½ cups water

Remove seeds but not peel from orange slices. Tie seeds in cheesecloth; set aside.

In a large bowl, cover orange slices with water. Let stand 48 hours. Change water 3 times. Drain; discard liquid.

Wash 5 (½ pint) jars in hot soapy water; rinse. Keep hot until needed. Prepare lids as manufacturer directs.

In a large saucepan, cover orange slices with water. Add salt. Cook over low heat until orange slices are transparent. Drain; discard liquid.

In a large saucepan, cook sugar and 7½ cups water over low heat until sugar dissolves, stirring continuously. Increase heat; boil 10 minutes. Add orange slices and bag of seeds. Bring to a boil again. Reduce heat; simmer 30 minutes. Remove from heat. Discard bag of seeds. Skim off foam. Cool 5 to 10 minutes.

Ladle hot jam into 1 hot jar at a time. Wipe rim of jar with a clean damp cloth. Attach lid. Fill and close remaining jars. Place in canner.

Process in a boiling water bath, page 13, 10 minutes.

Jam is runny.

Makes 5 (½ pints).

Four Fruit Jam

2 cups blackcurrants, stems removed

3 tablespoons water

2 cups redcurrants, stems removed

1½ cups raspberries, stems removed

1¼ cups strawberries, hulled

4 cups sugar

Wash 6 (½ pint) jars in hot, soapy water; rinse. Keep hot until needed. Prepare lids as manufacturer directs.

In a large saucepan, cook blackcurrants and water over low heat until blackcurrants are soft. Add redcurrants, raspberries, and strawberries. Cook 10 minutes. Add sugar. Stir until sugar dissolves. Increase heat; boil rapidly 10 to 15 minutes or until jam reaches 221F (105C). Remove from heat. Skim off foam. Cool 5 to 10 minutes.

Ladle hot jam into 1 hot jar at a time. Wipe rim of jar with a clean damp cloth. Attach lid. Fill and close remaining jars. Place in canner.

Process in a boiling water bath, page 13, 10 minutes.

Makes 6 (½ pints).

JELLIES

A quality jelly is clear and sparkling. It should retain its shape and quiver if removed from its jar. A good set depends upon the presence of sugar, pectin and acid in correct proportions. Follow the recipe carefully. Do not be tempted to hasten jelly making by squeezing the jelly bag or the result will be a cloudy jelly. Use as a spread on toast, bread, sweet rolls or muffins or as an accompaniment with meats.

Use sound, slightly under-ripe fruit which is not mushy. Wash and dry. Remove stems, leaves and any bruised parts. Prepare fruit according to recipe.

In a large saucepan, cook fruit and water, if necessary, over low heat until fruit is very soft.

Suspend a jelly bag over a large bowl. Pour mixture into jelly bag. Allow juice to drip slowly. Do not squeeze, stir or shake bag or jelly will be cloudy.

Measure juice. Weigh recommended quantity of sugar in proportion to juice.

In a large saucepan, warm juice. Add sugar. Cook over low heat, until sugar dissolves. Stir occasionally.

Increase heat. Boil rapidly until jelly reaches 221F (105C). Remove from heat. Skim off foam. Ladle hot jelly into hot jars. If using self-sealing lid, place hot lid on jar. Tighten screwband firmly. Invert jar 30 seconds. Stand jar upright to cool. Or, process in a boiling water bath, page 13, 5 minutes. If sealing with paraffin, see page 13.

Orange and Apple Jelly

4 oranges, coarsely chopped

3 lb. tart apples, coarsely chopped

7½ cups water

Sugar

In a large saucepan, simmer oranges, apples and water 1½ hours or until orange peel is very soft. Strain through a jelly bag. Measure liquid. Measure 2 cups sugar for each 2½ cups juice.

Wash 2 (½ pint) jars in hot soapy water; rinse. Keep hot until needed. Prepare lids as manufacturer directs.

In a large saucepan, cook juice over low heat. Add sugar. Stir until sugar dissolves. Increase heat; boil rapidly until jelly reaches 221F (105C).

Remove from heat. Skim off foam.

Ladle hot jelly into 1 hot jar at a time. Wipe rim of jar with a clean damp cloth. Attach lid. Fill and close remaining jars. Invert jars 30 seconds. Stand upright to cool. Or seal with paraffin, page 13.

Makes 2 (½ pints).

Blueberry and Apple Jelly

3 lb. blueberries, stems removed

3 lb. tart apples, coarsely chopped

Juice of 2 lemons

Sugar

In a large saucepan, place blueberries and apples. Just cover with water, simmer until fruit is soft. Using a wooden spoon, crush blueberries to release juice. Strain through a jelly bag. Measure juice. Measure 2 cups sugar for each 2½ cups juice.

Wash 3 (½ pint) jars in hot soapy water; rinse. Keep hot until needed. Prepare lids as manufacturer directs.

In a large saucepan, cook juice over low heat. Add lemon juice and sugar. Stir until sugar dissolves. Increase heat; boil rapidly until jelly reaches 221F (105C). Remove from heat. Skim off foam.

Ladle hot jelly into 1 hot jar at a time. Wipe rim of jar with a clean damp cloth. Attach lid. Fill and close remaining jars. Invert jars 30 seconds. Stand upright to cool. Or, seal with paraffin, page 13.

Makes 3 (½ pints).

Black Grape Jelly

3 lb. large sweet black grapes

Sugar

Remove grapes from stalks. In a large saucepan, simmer grapes until juice is released. Strain through a jelly bag. Measure juice. Measure 1½ cups sugar for each 2½ cups juice.

Wash 2 (½ pint) jars in hot soapy water; rinse. Keep hot until needed. Prepare lids as manufacturer directs.

In a large saucepan, simmer juice 10 minutes. Add sugar. Stir until sugar dissolves. Increase heat; boil rapidly until jelly reaches 221F (105C). Remove from heat. Skim off foam.

Ladle hot jelly into 1 hot jar at a time. Wipe rim of jar with a clean damp cloth. Attach lid. Fill and close remaining jars. Invert jars 30 seconds. Stand upright to cool. Or seal with paraffin, page 13.

Makes 2 (½ pints).

Blackcurrant Jelly

4 lb. blackcurrants, stems removed

7½ cups water

Sugar

In a large saucepan, simmer blackcurrants and water 1 hour or until blackcurrants are soft. Strain through a jelly bag. Measure juice. Measure 2 cups sugar for each 2½ cups juice.

Wash 6 (½ pint) jars in hot soapy water; rinse. Keep hot until needed. Prepare lids as manufacturer directs.

In a large saucepan, cook juice over low heat. Add sugar. Stir until sugar dissolves. Increase heat; boil rapidly until jelly reaches 221F (105C). Remove from heat. Skim off foam.

Ladle hot jelly into 1 hot jar at a time. Wipe rim of jar with a clean damp cloth. Attach lid. Fill and close remaining jars. Invert jars 30 seconds. Stand upright to cool. Or, seal with paraffin, page 13.

Makes 6 (½ pints).

Herb Jelly

3 lb. tart apples, chopped

6¼ cups water

1¼ cups white vinegar

Sugar

½ cup chopped fresh mint, tarragon, parsley or basil

Green food coloring

In a large saucepan, simmer apples, water and vinegar until apples are very soft. Strain through a jelly bag. Measure juice. Measure 2 cups sugar for each 2½ cups juice.

Wash 2 (½ pint) jars in hot soapy water; rinse. Keep hot until needed. Prepare vinegar-proof lids as manufacturer directs.

In a large saucepan, cook juice over low heat. Add sugar. Stir until sugar dissolves. Increase heat; boil rapidly 10-15 minutes, or until jelly reaches 221F (105C). Remove from heat. Stir in mint, tarragon, parsley or basil. Tint with food coloring as desired. Skim off foam.

Ladle hot jelly into 1 hot jar at a time. Wipe rim of jar with a clean damp cloth. Attach lid. Fill and close remaining jars. Invert jars 30 seconds. Stand upright to cool. Or, seal with paraffin, page 13.

Makes 2 (½ pints).

Cranberry and Apple Jelly

2 lb. cranberries

3 lb. tart apples, coarsely chopped

4 oranges, coarsely chopped

7½ cups water

Sugar

In a large saucepan, simmer cranberries, apples, oranges and water 1½ hours or until orange peel is soft. Strain through a jelly bag. Measure juice. Measure 2 cups sugar for each 2½ cups juice.

Wash 3 (½ pint) jars in hot soapy water; rinse. Keep hot until needed. Prepare lids as manufacturer directs.

In a large saucepan, cook juice over low heat. Add sugar. Stir until sugar dissolves. Increase heat; boil rapidly until jelly reaches 221F (105C). Remove from heat. Skim off foam.

Ladle hot jelly into 1 hot jar at a time. Wipe rim of jar with a clean damp cloth. Attach lid. Fill and close remaining jars. Invert jars 30 seconds. Stand upright to cool. Or, seal with paraffin, page 13.

Makes 3 (½ pints).

MARMALADES

Marmalade is a sweetened jelly made from citrus fruit and peel. Pectin, which is essential for a good set, exists in the pith and seeds of citrus fruit, so both are tied in a piece of cheesecloth and boiled with the peel. Use as a spread on toast or bread or as tart filling.

Wash and dry citrus fruit. *For thick-skinned fruit*, remove peel and white pith. Shred peel; coarsely chop fruit. *For thin-skinned fruit*, thinly slice whole fruit in quarters lengthwise, cut fruit and peel together in thin or thick strips.

Tie white pith and seeds into a piece of cheesecloth. Place in a large saucepan.

Simmer fruit, all juices and water 1 to 1½ hours or until peel is very soft. To check if peel is done, test a cooled piece between finger and thumb for softness. Remove seed bag, squeezing liquid back into pan; discard.

Add sugar. Stir until sugar dissolves.

Increase heat. Boil rapidly until marmalade reaches 221F (105C) or when a small amount of marmalade poured on a cool plate and left 1 minute wrinkles when pushed with a finger.

Let stand 10 minutes. Stir well to prevent peel rising. Ladle hot marmalade into hot jars, cover. Process in a boiling water bath, page 13, following recipe directions.

Oxford Marmalade

3 lb. Seville (bitter) oranges, halved, seeded

Juice of 1 lemon

12½ cups water

12 cups sugar

2 tablespoons molasses

4 tablespoons whiskey or rum, if desired

Squeeze juice from oranges. Cut oranges in thick shreds. In a large saucepan, simmer orange and lemon juice, shredded oranges and water 2 hours or until orange peel is soft. Add sugar and black molasses. Stir until sugar dissolves. Increase heat; boil rapidly 15 to 20 minutes or until marmalade reaches 221F (105C).

Remove from heat. Let stand 10 minutes. Add whiskey or rum, if desired.

Wash 12 (1 pint) jars in hot soapy water; rinse. Keep hot until needed. Prepare lids as manufacturer directs.

Stir well. Ladle hot marmalade into 1 hot jar at a time. Wipe rim of jar with a clean damp cloth. Attach lid. Fill and close remaining jars. Place in canner.

Process in a boiling water bath, page 13, 10 minutes.

Makes 12 (1 pints).

—— *Pineapple and Orange Marmalade* ——

3 oranges, thinly sliced crosswise, seeded

1 lemon, thinly sliced crosswise, seeded

2 x 1 lb. cans crushed pineapple in syrup

8 cups sugar

Quarter each citrus fruit slice. In a large saucepan, just cover citrus fruit with water. Simmer 45 minutes or until peel is soft. Add pineapple and syrup. Simmer 15 minutes. Add sugar. Stir until sugar dissolves. Increase heat; boil rapidly 20 to 25 minutes or until marmalade reaches 221F (105C).

Remove from heat. Let stand 10 minutes.

Wash 12 (½ pint) jars in hot soapy water; rinse. Keep hot until needed. Prepare lids as manufacturer directs.

Stir well. Ladle hot marmalade into 1 hot jar at a time. Wipe rim of jar with a clean damp cloth. Attach lid. Fill and close remaining jars. Place in canner.

Process in a boiling water bath, page 13, 10 minutes.

Makes 13 (½ pints).

Three Fruit Marmalade

2 grapefruit, quartered, seeded, peeled

2 oranges, quartered, seeded, peeled

4 lemons, quartered, seeded, peeled

15 cups water

12 cups sugar

Finely shred all citrus fruit peel. Remove thick white pith and membrane from grapefruit. Coarsely chop all citrus fruit pulp.

In a large saucepan, simmer peel, pulp and water 1½ hours. Add sugar. Stir until sugar dissolves. Increase heat; boil rapidly 15 to 20 minutes or until marmalade reaches 221F (105C).

Remove from heat. Let stand 10 minutes.

Wash 9 (1 pint) jars in hot soapy water; rinse. Keep hot until needed. Prepare lids as manufacturer directs.

Stir well. Ladle hot marmalade into 1 hot jar at a time. Wipe rim of jar with a clean damp cloth. Attach lid. Fill and close remaining jars. Place in canner.

Process in a boiling water bath, page 13, 10 minutes.

Makes 9 (1 pints).

Chunky Blender Marmalade

2 lb. Seville (bitter) oranges, quartered, seeded

1 lemon, quartered, seeded

10 cups water

8 cups sugar

In a food processor/blender, process oranges and lemon with ½ of water until finely chopped.

In a large saucepan, boil fruit and liquid and remaining water 1 hour. Reduce heat. Add sugar. Stir until sugar dissolves. Increase heat; boil rapidly 15 to 20 minutes or until marmalade reaches 221F (105C).

Remove from heat. Let stand 10 minutes.

Wash 13 (½ pint) jars in hot soapy water; rinse. Keep hot until needed. Prepare lids as manufacturer directs.

Stir well. Ladle hot marmalade into 1 hot jar at a time. Wipe rim of jar with a clean damp cloth. Attach lid. Fill and close remaining jars. Place in canner.

Process in a boiling water bath, page 13, 10 minutes.

Makes 13 (½ pints).

Lime Marmalade

Peel and juice of 12 limes

7½ cups water

6 cups sugar

Cut lime peel in very thin strips. Coarsely chop lime pulp. In a large saucepan, simmer peel, pulp, juice and water 1¼ hours or until peel is very soft. Add sugar. Stir until sugar dissolves. Increase heat; boil rapidly 10 to 15 minutes or until marmalade reaches 221F (105C).

Remove from heat. Let stand 10 minutes.

Wash 10 (½ pint) jars in hot soapy water; rinse. Keep hot until needed. Prepare lids as manufacturer directs.

Stir well. Ladle hot marmalade into 1 hot jar at a time. Wipe rim of jar with a clean damp cloth. Attach lid. Fill and close remaining jars. Place in canner.

Process in a boiling water bath, page 13, 10 minutes.

Makes 10 (½ pints).

Orange and Lemon Marmalade

4 oranges, thinly sliced crosswise, seeded

5 lemons, thinly sliced crosswise, seeded

12½ cups water

8 cups sugar

Quarter each citrus fruit slice. In a large saucepan, simmer citrus fruit and water 1½ hours. Add sugar. Stir until sugar dissolves. Increase heat; boil rapidly 10 to 15 minutes or until marmalade reaches 221F (105C).

Remove from heat. Let stand 10 minutes.

Wash 13 (½ pint) jars in hot, soapy water; rinse. Keep hot until needed. Prepare lids as manufacturer directs.

Stir well. Ladle hot marmalade into 1 hot jar at a time. Wipe rim of jar with a clean damp cloth. Attach lid. Fill and close remaining jars.

Process in a boiling water bath, page 13, 10 minutes.

Makes 13 (½ pints).

CURDS AND BUTTERS

Curds are thick creamy, fruit-flavored mixtures of eggs, butter and sugar with a 1 to 2 month storage life. Butters are thick mixtures of fruit pulp and sugar with a 6 month storage life. Serve curds and butters as a spread on cookies or bread, or as a tart filling.

In a heatproof bowl combine sugar, butter and fruit juice.

Strain in whole eggs. Place top of a double boiler or heatproof bowl over a pan of hot water.

Cook until mixture is thick and creamy. Stir constantly. Do not overcook. Ladle hot mixture into jars; cover. Process in a pressure canner, page 13, or a boiling water bath, page 13, following recipe directions.

Orange Curd with Candied Peel

Grated peel and juice of 4 large oranges

1 cup candied orange peel, chopped

1 cup sugar

1 cup sweet unsalted butter

6 egg yolks, beaten

Wash 3 (½ pint) jars in hot soapy water; rinse. Keep hot until needed. Prepare lids as manufacturer directs.

Strain orange juice. In top of a double boiler or a heatproof bowl set over a pan of simmering water, cook orange peel and juice, candied peel, sugar and butter until butter melts and sugar dissolves. Stir often. Stir in egg yolks, a little at a time. Cook until thick and creamy. Stir constantly. Do not overcook.

Ladle hot curd into 1 hot jar at a time. Wipe rim of jar with a clean damp cloth. Attach lid. Fill and close remaining jars. Place in canner.

Process in a pressure canner at 10 pounds pressure, page 13, 10 minutes.

Makes 3 (½ pints).

Spiced Apple Butter

3 lb. apples, coarsely chopped

2½ cups water

2½ cups hard cider

Light brown sugar

½ teaspoon ground cloves

½ teaspoon ground cinnamon

½ teaspoon ground nutmeg

In a large saucepan cook apples, water and cider over a low heat until apples are very soft. In a food processor/blender, process apples and liquid to a purée. Measure or weigh purée. Measure 1⅓ cups sugar for each 2 cups purée. Set aside.

Wash 8 (½ pint) jars in hot soapy water; rinse. Keep hot until needed. Prepare lids as manufacturer directs.

In a large saucepan, cook purée over low heat 30 to 40 minutes until mixture resembles thick cream. Add spices and sugar. Stir until sugar dissolves. Simmer gently, stirring often, until liquid evaporates.

Ladle hot butter into 1 hot jar at a time. Wipe rim of jar with a clean, damp cloth. Fill and close remaining jars. Place in canner.

Process in a boiling-water bath, page 13, 10 minutes.

Makes 8 (½ pints).

Thick Apricot Butter

3 cups dried apricots

1 orange

2 cups sugar

In a medium bowl, just cover apricots with water; let stand 12 hours.

In a large saucepan, cook apricots and liquid over medium heat until apricots are very soft. In a food processor/blender, process apricot and liquid to a purée. Set aside.

In a small saucepan, cover orange with water. Bring to a boil; cook until orange peel is very soft. Remove orange from pan; reserve liquid. Cool orange. Chop orange coarsely; discard seeds. In a food processor/blender, process chopped orange and reserved liquid.

Wash 3 (½ pint) jars in hot soapy water; rinse. Keep hot until needed. Prepare lids as manufacturer directs.

In a large saucepan, cook apricot and orange purées and sugar over low heat. Stir until sugar dissolves. Increase heat; boil until mixture resembles thick cream.

Ladle hot butter into 1 hot jar at a time. Wipe rim of jar with a clean, damp cloth. Attach lid. Fill and close remaining jars. Place in canner. Process in a boiling-water bath, page 13, 10 minutes.

Makes 3 (½ pints).

Soft Fruit Butter

4 cups blackcurrants, stems removed

4 cups redcurrants, stems removed

2¾ cups gooseberries, cleaned

3 cups strawberries, hulled

4 cups sugar

Wash 8 (½ pint) jars in hot soapy water; rinse. Keep hot until needed. Prepare lids as manufacturer directs.

In a large saucepan simmer all berries until juice runs from berries. Increase heat; cook 15 minutes. Reduce heat. Add sugar. Stir until sugar dissolves. Increase heat; boil rapidly 25 minutes or until very thick.

Ladle hot butter into 1 hot jar at a time. Wipe rim of jar with a clean, damp cloth. Attach lid. Fill and close remaining jars. Place in canner.

Process in a boiling water bath, page 13, 10 minutes.

Makes 8 (½ pints).

Rich Lemon Curd

2½ cups sugar cubes

Juice of 4 large lemons, strained

¾ cup sweet butter

7 eggs, beaten, strained

Wash 4 (½ pint) jars in hot soapy water; rinse. Keep hot until needed. Prepare lids as manufacturer directs.

Rub peel of lemons with sugar cubes. In a heat-proof bowl or top of double boiler set over a pan of hot water, place sugar cubes, lemon juice, butter and eggs over low heat until thick and creamy; stir constantly. Do not overcook.

Ladle hot curd into 1 hot jar at a time. Wipe rim of jar with a clean damp cloth. Attach lid. Fill and close remaining jars. Place in canner. Process in a pressure canner at 10 pounds pressure, page 13, 10 minutes.

Makes 4 (½ pints).

CONSERVES

Conserves are thick sweetened mixtures of fruit with such additions as dried fruit, nuts and spirits or liqueurs. Conserves may be served with cream, as a sauce for ice cream, used as tart fillings or as a spread.

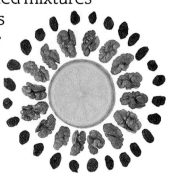

Prepare fruit according to recipe. In a large saucepan simmer fruit, sugar and water until fruit is soft.

Cook until thick. Conserves are more syrupy than jams and do not set. Stir in dried fruits, nuts and alcohol as directed.

Ladle hot conserve into hot jars; cover. Process in a boiling water bath, page 13, following recipe directions.

Pineapple Harlequin

1 (8 oz.) can crushed pineapple in syrup

2 cups dark sweet cherries, pitted

4 cups redcurrants, stems removed

2 oranges, thinly sliced, seeded, cored

3 cups raspberries, stems removed

Sugar

Drain pineapple; reserve syrup. In a large bowl, mix pineapple, cherries, redcurrants, raspberries and orange slices. Measure or weigh fruit. Measure 2¼ cups sugar for each 1 lb. fruit. Set aside.

In a large saucepan, cook fruit and reserved pineapple syrup. Add reserved sugar. Stir until sugar dissolves. Increase heat; boil rapidly 15 minutes until mixture thickens.

Wash 8 (½ pint) jars in hot soapy water; rinse. Keep hot until needed. Prepare lids as manufacturer directs.

Ladle hot mixture into 1 hot jar at a time. Wipe rim of jar with a clean damp cloth. Attach lid. Fill and close remaining jars. Place in canner.

Process in a boiling water bath, page 13, 10 minutes.

Makes 8 (½ pints).

Lemon Apples in Wine

Peel and juice of 8 lemons

2½ cups boiling water

2½ cups dry white wine

9 cups sugar

5 lb. eating apples, peeled, cored, sliced thinly

2 tablespoons brandy

In a large bowl, cover lemon peel with boiling water and wine. Let stand 30 minutes.

Wash 13 (½ pint) jars in hot soapy water; rinse. Keep hot until needed. Prepare lids as manufacturer directs.

In a large saucepan, cook peel and liquid, lemon juice and sugar over low heat. Stir until sugar dissolves. Increase heat; boil 10 minutes. Remove from heat. Strain liquid; return liquid to pan. Discard peel. Add apples. Cook over low heat until apples are soft and liquid resembles thin cream. Remove from heat. Stir in brandy.

Ladle hot mixture into 1 hot jar at a time. Wipe rim of jar with a clean damp cloth. Attach lids. Fill and close remaining jars. Place in canner.

Process in a boiling water bath, page 13, 10 minutes.

Makes 13 (½ pints).

Orange Walnut Conserve

2 lb. oranges

7½ cups water

½ cup raisins

4 cups sugar

½ cup walnuts, coarsely chopped

Finely grate orange peel; set aside. Remove remaining pith; discard. Chop flesh; discard seeds.

In a large saucepan cook orange flesh and water over low heat 30 minutes. Remove from heat. Measure 5 cups pulp. Add water if necessary to make correct measure.

Wash 6 (½ pint) jars in hot soapy water; rinse. Keep hot until needed. Prepare lids as manufacturer directs.

In a large saucepan, cook pulp, reserved peel, raisins and sugar, over low heat. Stir until sugar dissolves. Increase heat; boil rapidly 20 minutes. Stir in walnuts; bring to a boil again.

Ladle hot conserve into 1 hot jar at a time. Wipe rim of jar with a clean damp cloth. Attach lid. Fill and close remaining jars. Place in canner.

Process in a boiling water bath, page 13, 10 minutes.

Makes 6 (½ pints).

Plum, Rum and Raisin Conserve

4 lb. plums, halved, pitted

¾ cup raisins

1¼ cups water, if needed

6 cups sugar

1 cup blanched almonds, chopped

4 tablespoons dark rum

Wash 10 (½ pint) jars in hot soapy water; rinse. Keep hot until needed. Prepare lids as manufacturer directs.

In a large saucepan, simmer plums and raisins until plums are very soft. If plums are not juicy, add water.

Add sugar. Stir until sugar dissolves. Increase heat; boil rapidly until thickened. Remove from heat. Stir in almonds and rum.

Ladle hot conserve into 1 hot jar at a time. Wipe rim of jar with a clean damp cloth. Attach lid. Fill and close remaining jars. Place in canner.

Process in a boiling water bath, page 13, 10 minutes.

Makes 10 (½ pints).

Pear and Pineapple Conserve

2 lb. pears, peeled, cored, thinly sliced

1 cup water

2 cups sugar

1 small pineapple, peeled, coarsely grated

Wash 5 (½ pint) jars in hot soapy water; rinse. Keep hot until needed. Prepare lids as manufacturer directs.

In a large saucepan, bring pears, water and sugar to a boil over low heat. Add pineapple. Simmer 45 minutes.

Ladle hot conserve into 1 hot jar at a time. Wipe rim of jar with a clean damp cloth. Attach lid. Fill and close remaining jars. Place in canner.

Process in a boiling water bath, page 13, 10 minutes.

Makes 5 (½ pints).

FREEZER JAMS

Freezer jam has a fresher, more natural fruit taste and a brighter color than cooked jam. Both contain fruit or fruit juices, pectin and sugar. Fresh or frozen fruit can be used including strawberries, nectarines, peaches and apricots. Serve freezer jam as a spread on bread, toast or muffins, or as a tart filling.

Measure fresh or thawed frozen fruit exactly. In a large bowl, place fruit and sugar. Mash slightly. Let stand 20 minutes. Stir occasionally.

Add liquid pectin; stir 3 minutes.

Ladle jam into clean freezer containers; cover and label. Let stand 5 hours.

Refrigerate 24 to 48 hours or until jam
jells.

Store in freezer up to 6 months.

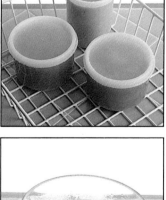

To serve, let stand 1 hour at room
temperature. Refrigerate leftover
jam. Use within 2 days.

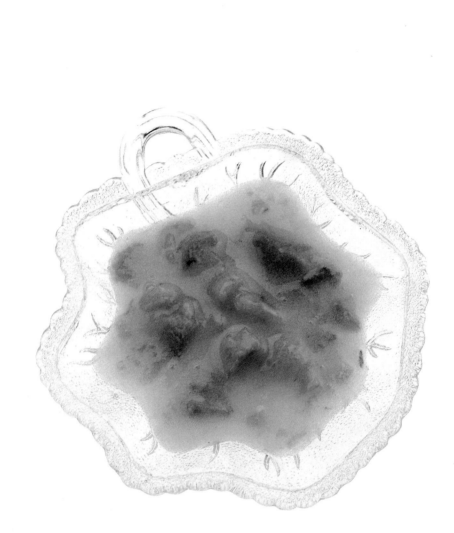

Freezer Nectarine Jam

1½ lb. ripe nectarines, peeled, pitted, coarsely chopped

4 cups superfine sugar

½ cup liquid pectin

1 teaspoon citric acid

Wash 6 (½ pint) freezer containers and lids in hot soapy water; rinse.

In a large bowl, mash nectarines well. Add sugar and citric acid. Let stand 20 minutes. Stir occasionally. Add liquid pectin; stir 3 minutes.

Ladle jam into prepared containers. Wipe rim of container with a clean damp cloth. Attach lid. Let stand 5 hours.

Refrigerate 24 to 48 hours or until jam jells. Store in freezer up to 6 months. To serve, let stand 1 hour at room temperature. Refrigerate leftover jam up to 2 days.

VARIATION: Fresh ripe peaches or apricots may also be used for this recipe.

Makes 6 (½ pint).

Freezer Strawberry Jam

5 cups strawberries, hulled, quartered

4 cups superfine sugar

½ cup liquid pectin

Wash 6 (½ pint) freezer containers and lids in hot soapy water; rinse.

In a large bowl, mash strawberries lightly using a fork. Add sugar. Let stand 20 minutes. Stir occasionally. Add liquid pectin; stir 3 minutes.

Ladle jam into prepared containers. Wipe rim of container with a clean damp cloth. Attach lid. Let stand 5 hours.

Refrigerate 24 to 48 hours or until jam jells. Store in freezer up to 6 months. To serve, let stand 1 hour at room temperature. Refrigerate leftover jam up to 2 days.

Makes 6 (½ pints).

MICROWAVE PRESERVES

Preserves and condiments can be made very successfully in a microwave oven, saving time and energy. The method is different to standard jam and chutney making, so follow the instructions carefully.

If fruit, such as raspberries, is frozen, defrost on low power 3 to 4 minutes or until soft.

Use a large microwave-safe bowl, 2 times volume of ingredients.

Add water, if necessary. Lightly cover. Microwave on full power for time specified in recipe.

Stir in sugar. Microwave uncovered on full power for specified time, stirring occasionally.

Test for setting, page 12.

Stir well. Cool 5 minutes. Stir again. Pour into hot jars; cover. Process in a pressure canner, page 13, or in a boiling water bath, page 13, according to recipe directions.

Microwave Raspberry Jam

3 cups raspberries

2 tablespoons lemon juice

2 cups sugar

Wash 3 (½ pint) jars in hot soapy water; rinse. Keep hot until needed. Prepare lids as manufacturer directs.

In a large microwave-safe bowl, microwave raspberries, lemon juice and sugar on full power 5 minutes, stirring occasionally until sugar dissolves. Microwave on full power 12 minutes or until jam reaches 221F (105C). Let stand 5 minutes.

Stir well. Ladle hot jam into 1 hot jar at a time. Wipe rim of jar with a clean damp cloth. Attach lid. Fill and close remaining jars, place in canner.

Process in a boiling water bath, page 13, 10 minutes.

Makes 3 (½ pints).

Microwave Lemon Curd

½ cup butter

Grated peel and juice of 3 large lemons

1 cup sugar

3 eggs, beaten

1 egg yolk, beaten

Wash 2 (½ pint) jars in hot soapy water; rinse. Keep hot until needed. Prepare lids as manufacturer directs.

In a large microwave-safe bowl, microwave butter and lemon peel and juice on full power 3 minutes. Stir in sugar. Microwave 2 minutes. Stir in eggs and egg yolk, a little at a time. Microwave on low power 12 to 15 minutes or until curd thickens, stirring occasionally.

Ladle hot curd into 1 hot jar at a time. Wipe rim of jar with a clean damp cloth. Attach lid. Fill and close remaining jars. Place in canner.

Process in a pressure canner, page 13, at 10 pounds pressure 10 minutes.

Makes 2 (½ pints).

Microwave Spiced Oranges

5 Valencia oranges, sliced thinly crosswise

1¼ cups water

1¼ cups white wine vinegar

1½ cups sugar

1 (2-inch) cinnamon stick

6 to 10 whole cloves

In a large microwave-safe bowl, microwave oranges and water, tightly covered, on full power 15 to 20 minutes or until orange peel is very soft. Drain; discard water.

In a medium microwave-safe bowl, microwave vinegar, sugar and cinnamon on full power 10 minutes, stirring occasionally until sugar dissolves.

Add orange slices. Microwave, tightly covered, on low power 25 to 30 minutes or until orange peel is transparent.

Wash 2 (½ pint) jars in hot soapy water; rinse. Keep hot until needed. Prepare vinegar-proof lids as manufacturer directs.

Place 3 to 5 cloves in each hot jar. Using a slotted spoon, pack orange slices into hot jars.

Microwave remaining syrup on full power 7 minutes. Strain syrup. Ladle hot syrup over orange slices. Wipe rim of jars with a clean damp cloth. Attach vinegar-proof lids. Place in canner.

Process in a boiling water bath, page 13, 10 minutes.

Makes 2 (½ pints).

Microwave Cucumber Relish

2 large cucumbers, chopped

2 medium onions, finely chopped

2 tablespoons non-iodized salt

1¼ cups white vinegar

⅓ cup sugar

½ teaspoon celery seeds

½ teaspoon mustard seeds

In a medium bowl, combine cucumber, onions and salt. Let stand 2 hours. Rinse under cold running water; drain. Set aside.

Wash 2 (½ pint) jars in hot soapy water; rinse. Keep hot until needed. Prepare vinegar-proof lids as manufacturer directs.

In a large microwave-safe bowl, microwave vinegar, sugar and celery and mustard seeds on full power 6 minutes, stirring 2 to 3 times. Stir in cucumber mixture. Microwave on full power 2 minutes.

Ladle hot relish into 1 hot jar at a time. Wipe rim of jar with a clean damp cloth. Attach lid. Fill and close remaining jar. Place in canner.

Process in a boiling water bath, page 13, 5 minutes. Let mature 1 month before using.

Makes 2 (½ pints).

PICKLES

Pickled fruits and vegetables and relishes are products with crisp, sour or sweet-sour flavor. Good quality vinegar is essential for pickling. Choose a vinegar containing at least 5% acetic acid or it will not preserve fruit or vegetables. Use pickles and relishes as an accompaniment with meats or with curries or spicy foods.

Use fruit and vegetables of high quality. Avoid soft fruit and vegetables. Prepare by chopping or slicing according to recipe.

If specified in recipe, soak vegetables in brine using 2 cups salt to 7 cups water, or ¾ cup salt to 1 ½ lb. vegetables. Let stand 24 hours to withdraw some natural juices which dilute preserving vinegar.

Drain. Rinse under cold running water. Drain thoroughly. If using fruit, cook in liquid as directed.

Prepare spiced or sweetened vinegar.

Add fruit or vegetables to vinegar and cook for specified time.

Pack hot fruit or vegetables and vinegar mixture into hot jars; cover with vinegar-proof lids. Process in a boiling water bath, page 13.

Spiced Prunes

3 cups large prunes

2 cups cold steeped tea

2½ cups white wine vinegar

2 cups sugar

1 (1-inch) cinnamon stick

1 teaspoon cloves

10 allspice berries

Blade of mace

In a large bowl, cover prunes with tea. Let stand 12 hours.

Wash 2 (1 pint) jars in hot soapy water; rinse. Keep hot until needed. Prepare vinegar-proof lids as manufacturer directs.

In a large saucepan, cook prunes and liquid over low heat 15 to 20 minutes until prunes are plump.

In a large saucepan, bring vinegar, sugar and spices to a boil. Reduce heat; simmer 5 minutes. Add prunes and liquid. Simmer 5 minutes. Using a slotted spoon, pack hot prunes into hot jars.

Increase heat; bring syrup to a boil. Ladle hot syrup over prunes. Wipe rim of jars with a clean damp cloth. Attach lids. Place in canner. Process in a boiling water bath, page 13, 20 minutes. Let mature 1 week before using.

Makes 2 (1 pints).

Pickled Eggplants

4 lb. eggplants, peeled, cut in julienne pieces

4 tablespoons salt

4½ cups white wine vinegar

2 tablespoons sugar

½ cup olive oil

3 tablespoon chopped fresh chives

2 tablespoons chopped fresh marjoram or oregano

2 dried chili peppers

8 garlic cloves, halved

Wash 4 (1 pint) jars in hot soapy water; rinse. Keep hot until needed. Prepare vinegar-proof lids as manufacturer directs.

Place eggplants in a colander. Sprinkle with salt. Shake colander. Drain 30 minutes. In a large saucepan bring vinegar and sugar to a boil. Add eggplants. Bring to a boil. Reduce heat; simmer 5 minutes. Drain. Reserve liquid.

Mix hot eggplants, olive oil, chives and marjoram or oregano. Pack into hot jars. Add 1 chili pepper and 4 garlic pieces to each jar. Using a wooden spoon, press eggplants to release juice. Ladle reserved liquid over eggplants. Wipe rim of jars with a clean damp cloth. Attach lids. Place in canner. Process in a boiling water bath, page 13, 15 minutes.

Let mature 1 month before using.

Makes 4 (1 pints).

Chow Chow

1 lb. cucumbers, peeled, diced

1 lb. onions, chopped

1 lb. green tomatoes, chopped

1 lb. green beans, chopped

1 lb. celery, finely chopped

1 lb. small cauliflower flowerets

1 lb. hard white cabbage, shredded

4 tablespoons non-iodized salt

5 cups malt vinegar

1 cup sugar

5 tablespoons dry mustard

3 tablespoons all-purpose flour

1 tablespoon turmeric

In a large bowl, combine all vegetables. Sprinkle with salt. Cover with cold water. Let stand 24 hours. Drain. Add ½ of vinegar. Let stand 12 hours.

In a small bowl, mix sugar, mustard, flour, turmeric and a small amount of remaining vinegar. In a large saucepan, bring remaining vinegar to a boil. Stir in mustard mixture. Reduce heat; simmer 2 minutes. Add vegetables and liquid. Increase heat; bring to a boil. Simmer 20 minutes, stirring often.

Wash 6 (1 pint) jars in hot soapy water; rinse. Keep hot until needed. Prepare vinegar-proof lids as manufacturer directs.

Pack hot Chow Chow into 1 hot jar at a time. Wipe rim of jar with a clean damp cloth. Attach lid. Fill and close remaining jars. Place in canner. Process in a boiling water bath, page 13, 5 minutes. Let mature 1 month before using.

Makes 6 (1 pints).

Brown Sugar Pickled Peaches

2 lb. small firm peaches, peeled

1¼ cups white wine vinegar

2 cups light brown sugar

1 (1-inch) cinnamon stick

6 whole cloves

Wash 5 (½ pint) jars in hot soapy water; rinse. Keep hot until needed. Prepare vinegar-proof lids as manufacturer directs.

In a large saucepan, cook vinegar, sugar and spices over low heat. Stir until sugar dissolves. Add peaches. Increase heat; bring to a boil. Reduce heat; simmer until peaches are soft but not broken.

Using a slotted spoon, pack hot peaches in hot jars.

Increase heat; bring syrup to a boil. Ladle hot syrup over peaches. Wipe rim of jars with a clean damp cloth. Attach lids. Place in canner.

Process in a boiling water bath, page 13, 20 minutes. Let mature 3 months before using.

Makes 5 (½ pints).

Italian Fruit Mustard Pickles

3½ cups sugar

1 cup water

2 lb. mixed fruit, (peaches, apricots, plums, cherries, figs and melons), peeled, pitted, chopped

⅔ cup white wine vinegar

4 tablespoons mustard powder

In a large saucepan, cook 3 cups sugar and water over low heat 15 minutes or until sugar dissolves. Add fruit. Simmer 15 minutes or until fruit is soft but not broken. Remove from heat; cool.

In a small saucepan, cook remaining sugar and vinegar over low heat 15 minutes. Remove from heat; cool. Mix in mustard. Let stand 1 hour.

Wash 5 (½ pint) jars in hot soapy water; rinse. Keep hot until needed. Prepare vinegar-proof lids as manufacturer directs.

Stir mustard syrup into fruit. Pack hot fruit into hot jars. Ladle hot syrup over fruit. Wipe rim of jars with a clean damp cloth. Attach lids. Place in canner. Process in a boiling water bath, page 13, 20 minutes. Let mature 24 hours. Store up to 6 months.

Makes 5 (½ pints).

Pickled Dill Cucumbers

7 lb. pickling cucumbers, about 3 inches long

4½ cups cider vinegar

7 cups sugar

2 tablespoons non-iodized salt

2 tablespoons mixed pickling spice

2 tablespoons dill seed

In a large bowl, cover cucumber with boiling water. Let stand 24 hours. Drain. Repeat process 3 days. Use fresh water each time.

In a large saucepan, bring vinegar, sugar, salt and pickling spice to a boil. Pour over cucumbers. Let stand 24 hours. Drain. Reserve liquid.

Wash 10 (1 pint) jars in hot soapy water; rinse. Keep hot until needed. Prepare vinegar-proof lids as manufacturer directs.

In a large saucepan, bring reserved liquid to a boil. Add cucumbers. Bring to the boil. Pack hot cucumbers into hot jars. Divide dill seed between jars. Bring liquid again to a boil. Ladle hot liquid over cucumbers. Wipe rim of jars with a clean damp cloth. Attach lids. Place in canner. Process in a boiling water bath, page 13, 10 minutes. Let mature 2 weeks before using.

Makes 10 (1 pints).

Pickled Pears

4 cups sugar

2½ cups white wine vinegar

1½ tablespoons whole cloves

1½ tablespoons whole allspice

Large piece of dried gingerroot, mashed

1 (3-inch) cinnamon stick

Grated peel of ½ lemon

4 lb. small pears, peeled, cored, quartered

In a large saucepan, cook sugar and vinegar over low heat. Stir until sugar dissolves . Tie cloves, allspice, gingerroot, cinnamon stick and lemon peel in a piece of muslin. Suspend in pan so spices are immersed in liquid. Add pears. Simmer 40 minutes or until pears are soft but not broken.

Wash 4 (1 pint) jars in hot soapy water; rinse. Keep hot until needed. Prepare vinegar-proof lids as manufacturer directs.

Using a slotted spoon, pack hot pears in hot jars. Discard spice bag. Increase heat; boil syrup 10 minutes or until syrupy. Ladle hot syrup over pears. Wipe rim of jars with a clean damp cloth. Attach lids. Place in canner. Process in a boiling water bath, page 13, 20 minutes.

Let mature 1 month before using.

Makes 4 (1 pints).

Pickled Lemons

12 lemons

2 tablespoons non-iodized salt

3¾ cups white wine vinegar

12 white peppercorns

Large piece of dried gingerroot, mashed

3 tablespoons white mustard seeds

2 garlic cloves, crushed

Using a sharp knife, cut skins of lemons lengthwise without cutting pulp. Rub salt into cuts. In a shallow bowl, let lemons stand 5 days in a cool place. Turn lemons occasionally. Drain; reserve liquid. In a large saucepan, bring reserved liquid, vinegar, peppercorns and ginger to a boil. Reduce heat; simmer 5 minutes. Add lemons. Simmer 30 minutes.

Wash 5 (½ pint) jars in hot soapy water; rinse. Keep hot until needed. Prepare vinegar-proof lids as manufacturer directs.

Using a slotted spoon, pack hot lemons in hot jars. Add mustard seeds and garlic to liquid. Increase heat; bring to a boil. Remove ginger. Skim off foam. Ladle hot liquid over lemons. Wipe rim of jars with a clean damp cloth. Attach lids. Place in canner. Process in a boiling water bath, page 13, 5 minutes.

Let mature 1 month before using.

Makes 5 (½ pints).

CHUTNEYS

Chutney is a condiment that is made of fruits or vegetables cooked in vinegar, sweetened with sugar or dried fruit and flavored with spices. Chutneys should be smooth and pulpy with a mellow flavor and are best left to mature to blend flavors for at least one month. Use as an accompaniment with meats, curries, cheese, and savory pies or as a filling for sandwiches.

Prepare fruit and vegetables according to recipe. Remove all bruises. Chop finely, mince, or process in a food processor/blender.

In a large saucepan cook fruit, dried fruit, vegetables and vinegar over low heat to soften ingredients and break down fibers.

Add remaining vinegar, sugar and spices.

Cook over low heat, stirring often, 1 hour or until chutney is thick and golden brown with no excess liquid.

Remove from heat. Stir well. Ladle or pour hot chutney into hot jars; cover with vinegar-proof lids. Process in a boiling water bath, page 13, 20 minutes.

Let mature to blend flavors 1 month before using.

Mixed Fruit Chutney

1 lb. plums, halved, pitted. roughly chopped

2 lb. tomatoes, peeled, coarsely chopped

4 lb. tart apples, peeled, cored, finely chopped

2 lb. ripe pears, peeled, cored, finely chopped

10⅔ cups dark brown sugar

2 cups seedless raisins

5 cups malt vinegar

1½ tablespoons salt

1 teaspoon ground black pepper

1 teaspoon ground ginger

1 teaspoon ground cloves

1 teaspoon ground mace

1 teaspoon cayenne pepper

In a large saucepan, mix plums, tomatoes, apples and pears. Stir in sugar, raisins, vinegar, salt and spices. Bring to a boil, stirring well. Reduce heat; simmer 1¼ hours or until thick and golden brown. Stir often.

Wash 10 (1 pint) jars in hot soapy water; rinse. Keep hot until needed. Prepare vinegar-proof lids as manufacturer directs.

Ladle hot chutney into 1 hot jar at a time. Wipe rim of jar with clean damp cloth. Attach lid. Fill and close remaining jars. Place in canner. Process in a boiling water bath, page 13, 20 minutes. Let mature 1 month before using.

Makes 10 (1 pints).

Apple Ginger Chutney

3 lb. tart apples, peeled, cored, finely chopped

2 cups light brown sugar

2½ cups cider vinegar

1½ tablespoons salt

1½ teaspoons ground ginger

1 teaspoon ground allspice

1 teaspoon ground cloves

1 green pepper, finely chopped

1 medium onion, finely chopped

½ cup preserved ginger in syrup, finely chopped

½ cup golden raisins

Grated peel and juice of ½ lemon

In a large saucepan, bring apples, sugar, vinegar, salt and spices to a boil, stirring well. Reduce heat; simmer 10 minutes. Add pepper, onion, ginger and syrup, raisins and lemon peel and juice. Increase heat; bring to a boil. Reduce heat; simmer 1 hour or until thick and golden brown. Stir often.

Wash 3 (1 pint) jars in hot soapy water; rinse. Keep hot until needed. Prepare vinegar-proof lids as manufacturer directs.

Ladle hot chutney into 1 hot jar at a time. Wipe rim of jar with a clean damp cloth. Attach lid. Fill and close remaining jars. Place in canner. Process in a boiling water bath, page 13, 20 minutes. Let mature 1 month before using.

Makes 3 (1 pints).

Sweet Grape Chutney

2 lb. white grapes, halved, seeded

2 lb. tart apples, peeled, cored, finely chopped

3⅓ cups light brown sugar

1 cup golden raisins

1¼ cups cider vinegar

⅔ cups lemon juice

Grated peel of ½ lemon

½ teaspoon ground allspice

½ teaspoon ground cloves

½ teaspoon salt

¼ teaspoon ground cinnamon

Pinch of paprika

In a large saucepan, bring all ingredients to a boil, stirring well. Reduce heat; simmer 1 hour or until thick and golden brown. Stir often.

Wash 3 (1 pint) jars in hot soapy water; rinse. Keep hot until needed. Prepare vinegar-proof lids as manufacturer directs.

Ladle hot chutney into 1 hot jar at a time. Wipe rim of jar with a clean damp cloth. Attach lid. Fill and close remaining jars. Place in canner. Process in a boiling water bath, page 13, 20 minutes.

Let mature 1 month before using.

Makes 3 (1 pints).

Lemon Chutney

6 large lemons, thinly sliced crosswise, seeded

½ lb. onions, finely chopped

1½ tablespoons non-iodized salt

Water

2 cups cider vinegar

1⅓ cups light brown sugar

½ cup golden raisins

1½ tablespoons white mustard seeds

1 teaspoon ground ginger

½ teaspoon cayenne pepper

In a large bowl, mix lemon slices and onions. Sprinkle with salt. Let stand 24 hours.

Wash 3 (½ pint) jars in hot soapy water; rinse. Keep hot until needed. Prepare vinegar-proof lids as manufacturer directs.

In a large saucepan, place lemons, onions and liquid. Just cover with water, cook over low heat until lemon peel is soft but not broken. Add vinegar, sugar, raisins and spices. Increase heat; bring to a boil, stirring well. Reduce heat; simmer 1 hour or until thick and golden brown. Stir often.

Ladle hot chutney into 1 hot jar at a time. Wipe rim of jar with a clean damp cloth. Attach lid. Fill and close remaining jars. Place in canner. Process in a boiling water bath, page 13, 20 minutes. Let mature 1 month before using.

Makes 3 (½ pints).

Banana Chutney

8 large ripe bananas, peeled, thinly sliced

1 lb. onions, finely chopped

1¼ cups dates, pitted, chopped

½ cup crystallized ginger, chopped

2½ cups cider vinegar

1⅓ cups light brown sugar

1 tablespoon salt

1 tablespoon mixed pickling spice

Wash 2 (1 pint) jars in hot soapy water; rinse. Keep hot until needed. Prepare vinegar-proof lids as manufacturer directs.

In a large saucepan, mix bananas, onions, dates, ginger, vinegar, sugar and salt. Tie pickling spice in a 6-inch square of cheesecloth. Suspend in pan so spices are immersed in liquid. Bring to a boil. Reduce heat; simmer 1 hour or until thick and golden brown. Stir often.

Remove cheesecloth. Ladle hot chutney into 1 hot jar at a time. Wipe rim of jar with a clean damp cloth. Attach lid. Fill and close remaining jars. Place in canner. Process in a boiling water bath, page 13, 20 minutes. Let mature 1 month before using.

Makes 2 (1 pints).

Mango Chutney

6 ripe mangoes, peeled, thinly sliced

1¼ cups cider vinegar

1⅓ cups light brown sugar

1½ oz. fresh gingerroot, peeled, chopped

2 garlic cloves, crushed

2 teaspoons chili powder

1 teaspoon salt

In a large saucepan, cook mangoes and vinegar over low heat 10 minutes. Stir in sugar, ginger, garlic, chili powder and salt. Increase heat; bring slowly to a boil, stirring well. Reduce heat; simmer 30 minutes. Stir occasionally.

Wash 1 (½ pint) jar in hot soapy water; rinse. Keep hot until needed. Prepare vinegar-proof lids as manufacturer directs.

Ladle hot chutney into 1 hot jar at a time. Wipe rim of jar with a clean damp cloth. Attach lid. Fill and close remaining jars. Place in canner. Process in a boiling water bath, page 13, 20 minutes. Let mature 1 month before using.

Makes 1 (½ pint).

Mint Chutney

5 lb. tart apples, peeled, cored, finely chopped

2⅔ cups light brown sugar

2½ cups cider vinegar

2 cups onions, chopped

1¼ cups dates, pitted, chopped

1 cup golden raisins

1 tablespoon salt

1 tablespoon ground ginger

4 tablespoons fresh mint, finely chopped

In a large saucepan, bring all ingredients except mint to a boil, stirring well. Reduce heat; simmer 1¼ hours or until thick and golden brown. Stir often. Stir in mint.

Wash 6 (1 pint) jars in hot water; rinse. Keep hot until needed. Prepare vinegar-proof lids as manufacturer directs.

Ladle hot chutney into 1 hot jar at a time. Wipe rim of jar with a clean damp cloth. Attach lid. Fill and close remaining jars. Place in canner. Process in a boiling water bath, page 13, 15 minutes.

Let mature 1 month before using.

Makes 6 (1 pints).

Apricot Chutney

2 lb. apricots, peeled, pitted, chopped

1 lb. onions, finely chopped

2⅔ cups dark brown sugar

2½ cups white wine vinegar

1 cup preserved ginger, chopped

Grated peel and juice of 1 orange

1½ tablespoons salt

2 teaspoons white mustard seeds

1 teaspoon cayenne pepper

½ teaspoon ground turmeric

1 cup walnut halves

In a large saucepan, mix apricots, onions, sugar and vinegar. Stir in ginger, orange peel and juice, salt and spices. Bring to a boil. Reduce heat; simmer 1 hour or until thick and golden brown. Stir often.

Wash 3 (1 pint) jars in hot soapy water; rinse. Keep hot until needed. Prepare lids as manufacturer directs.

Stir walnut halves into chutney. Ladle hot chutney into 1 hot jar at a time. Wipe rim of jar with a clean damp cloth. Attach lid. Fill and close remaining jars. Place in canner. Process in a boiling water bath, page 13, 20 minutes. Let mature 1 month before using.

Makes 3 (1 pints).

SAUCES & CATSUPS

Sauces and catsups are condiments or relishes for food. Serve as an accompaniment with meats, poultry or savory pies or use in the preparation of savory dishes.

Prepare fruit and/or vegetables according to recipe.

In a large saucepan, cook vinegar, sugar and flavoring ingredients over low heat until fruit and vegetables are very soft.

Strain through a sieve. Press through as much purée as possible.

Cook over low heat, stirring frequently, until mixture is thick and smooth.

Pour into hot sterilized bottles, attach vinegar-proof lids.

Process in a boiling water bath, page 13.

Mixed Fruit Sauce

3 lb. red or green tomatoes, coarsely chopped

3 lb. cooking apples, peeled, cored, chopped

1 lb. onions, chopped

4 cups raisins

1½ cups dates, chopped

3¾ cups white vinegar

2 teaspoons salt

1 teaspoon ground mixed spice, ground ginger and mustard powder

½ teaspoon ground cloves

½ teaspoon cayenne pepper

Pinch of ground mace and chili powder

4 cups light brown sugar

In a large saucepan, bring tomatoes, apples, onions, raisins, dates, vinegar, salt and spices to a boil. Reduce heat; simmer 1 hour or until fruit and vegetables are soft. Strain through a sieve. In a large saucepan, cook purée and sugar over low heat. Stir until sugar dissolves. Increase heat; bring to a boil. Reduce heat; simmer 45 minutes or until thick.

Wash 8 (½ pint) jars in hot soapy water; rinse. Keep hot until needed. Prepare vinegar-proof lids as manufacturer directs.

Ladle hot sauce into 1 hot jar at a time. Wipe rim of jar with a clean damp cloth. Attach lid. Fill and close remaining jars. Place in canner. Process in a boiling water bath, page 13, 30 minutes.

Makes 8 (½ pints).

Walnut Catsup

80 green walnuts, casings split

7½ cups vinegar

½ lb. onions, chopped

1½ cups non-iodized salt

1 tablespoon black peppercorns

1 tablespoon allspice berries

12 whole cloves

6 blades of mace

Use walnuts before shells form inside green casing. In a food processor/blender, process walnuts. In a large saucepan, bring vinegar, onions, salt and spices to a boil.

In a large bowl, cover processed walnuts with boiling liquid. Cover; let stand 14 days in a cold place. Stir each day. Strain through a jelly bag. In a large saucepan, bring strained liquid to a boil. Simmer 1 hour.

Wash 5 (½ pint) jars in hot soapy water; rinse. Keep hot until needed. Prepare vinegar-proof lids as manufacturer directs.

Ladle hot vinegar into 1 hot jar at a time. Wipe rim of jar with clean damp cloth. Attach lid. Fill and close remaining jars. Place in canner. Process in a boiling water bath, page 13, 30 minutes. Add to soups, stews and casseroles.

Makes 5 (½ pints).

Mushroom Catsup

2 lb. large, dark, open mushrooms

¾ cup non-iodized salt

2½ cups vinegar

1 (2-inch) piece of dried gingerroot

6 blades of mace

4 whole cloves

1 teaspoon allspice

1 teaspoon black peppercorns

1 (1-inch) cinnamon stick

Cut off bottom of mushroom stalks; discard. Break mushrooms and stalks into small pieces. In a large ovenware bowl layer mushrooms and salt. Cover. Let stand in cool place 5 days. Stirring each day.

Preheat oven to 300F (150C). Cover mushrooms and liquid with foil. Bake in preheated oven 1½ hours. Strain through a jelly bag. In a large saucepan, bring liquid, vinegar, gingerroot and spices to a boil. Reduce heat; simmer until liquid is reduced ½. Strain through a jelly bag. In a large saucepan bring liquid to a boil.

Wash 2 (½ pint) jars in hot soapy water; rinse. Keep hot until needed. Prepare vinegar-proof lids as manufacturer directs.

Ladle hot vinegar into 1 hot jar at a time, leaving ¼-inch headspace. Wipe rim of jar with a clean damp cloth. Attach lid. Fill and close remaining jars. Place in canner. Process in a boiling water bath, page 13, 30 minutes.

Makes 2 (½ pints).

Spiced Cranberry Sauce

4 lb. cranberries

1 lb. onions, finely chopped

2 cups water

2 cups sugar

1¼ cups cider vinegar

2 tablespoons salt

1 teaspoon ground cloves

1 teaspoon ground cinnamon

1 teaspoon ground allspice

1 teaspoon ground black pepper

In a large saucepan, cook cranberries, onions and water, covered, over low heat 30 minutes or until cranberries and onions are soft. Press through a sieve. Return juice to pan. Stir in sugar, vinegar, salt and spices. Cook over a low heat. Stir until sugar dissolves. Increase heat; bring to boil. Reduce heat; simmer 20 minutes.

Wash 5 (½ pint) jars in hot soapy water; rinse. Keep hot until needed. Prepare vinegar-proof lids as manufacturer directs.

Ladle hot sauce into 1 hot jar at a time. Wipe rim of jar with a clean damp cloth. Attach lid. Fill and close remaining jars. Place in canner. Process in a boiling water bath, page 13, 30 minutes.

Makes 5 (½ pints).

Tomato Sauce

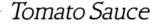

8 lb. ripe tomatoes, coarsely chopped

4 large onions, coarsely chopped

4 cups light brown sugar

5 cups vinegar

6 tablespoons black peppercorns

3 tablespoons salt

1 teaspoon ground cloves

1 teaspoon cayenne pepper

In a large saucepan, simmer all ingredients 2 hours. Stir occasionally. Strain through a sieve. In a large saucepan, bring purée to a boil. Boil 5 minutes.

Wash 7 (½ pint) jars in hot soapy water; rinse. Keep hot until needed. Prepare vinegar-proof lids as manufacturer directs.

Ladle hot sauce into 1 hot jar at a time. Wipe rim of jar with a clean damp cloth. Attach lid. Fill and close remaining jars. Place in canner. Process in a boiling water bath, page 13, 30 minutes.

Makes 7 (½ pints).

Plum Sauce

2 lb. plums, coarsely chopped

1 cup sugar

2½ cups vinegar

1 teaspoon salt

1 teaspoon ground ginger

½ teaspoon cayenne pepper

¼ teaspoon ground cloves

In a large saucepan, cook plums and pits over low heat 10 minutes. Add remaining ingredients. Increase heat; bring to a boil. Reduce heat; simmer 30 minutes. Press through a sieve. Return juice to pan. Cook over low heat 30 minutes. Stir occasionally.

Wash 5 (½ pint) jars in hot soapy water; rinse. Keep hot until needed. Prepare vinegar-proof lids as manufacturer directs.

Ladle hot sauce into 1 hot jar at a time. Wipe rim of jar with a clean damp cloth. Attach lids. Fill and close remaining jars. Place in canner. Process in a boiling water bath, page 13, 30 minutes.

Makes 5 (½ pint).

FRUIT IN ALCOHOL

Fruit in alcohol improves when kept, so allow the fruit to mellow at least one month before serving. The fruit will keep for one year. Serve as a dessert with cream or yogurt or add to a fresh fruit salad.

Prepare fresh, high quality ripe fruit according to recipe. Prepare spices.

Place fruit, spices and sugar in clean, hot jars. Pour wine, brandy or rum over fruit; top up with water. Put on tops of jars, but not screwbands.

Place jars in 250F (130C) oven and leave for 3 hours. Remove from oven and screw on tops tightly. Cool and store.

Mulled Pears in Red Wine

6 lb. small, unripe pears

2¼ cups sugar

Peel of 1 lemon, cut in thin strips

1 bottle red wine

1 teaspoon whole cloves

1 (6-inch) cinnamon stick, cut in pieces

4 blades of mace

2 (3-inch) pieces gingerroot, bruised

Water

Wash 2 (3 quart) jars and lids in hot soapy water; rinse. Keep hot until needed.

Carefully peel whole pears retaining stalks. Pack into prepared jars. Divide sugar among jars.

Place a strip of lemon peel into each jar, and divide cloves, cinnamon stick, mace blades and ginger between jars. Pour wine over pears and top up jars with water. Put on tops of the jars but not screwbands. Place in 250F (130C) oven and leave for 3 hours. Remove from oven and screw on tops tightly. Cool and store.

Makes 2 (3 quarts).

Brandied Apricots

6 lb. ripe apricots, peeled

4 lb. sugar

6¼ cups water

Brandy

Wash 6 (1 pint) jars and lids in hot soapy water; rinse. Keep hot until needed.

In a large saucepan, cook sugar and water over low heat. Stir until sugar dissolves. Increase heat; bring to a boil. Boil 10 minutes without stirring. Add apricots to syrup a few at a time. Reduce heat; simmer for 5 minutes until apricots are soft but not broken. Using a slotted spoon, pack apricots into a hot warm jar. Simmer syrup until syrup resembles thin cream. Measure syrup. Measure an equal amount of brandy. Return syrup to pan. Increase heat; bring to a boil. Remove from heat. Stir in brandy. Ladle syrup over apricots. Cover tightly.

VARIATION: Substitute peaches for apricots.

Makes 6 (1 pints).

Everlasting Rumpot

Mixed fruit, (strawberries, cherries, apricots, peaches, raspberries, plums, redcurrants, grapes or melon)

Sugar, equal to weight of fruit

Light or dark rum

Wash a jar or jars and lid or lids in hot soapy water; rinse.

Do not use citrus fruit, apples, pears or bananas. Use sound ripe fruit, just a few pieces of each type, and wipe fruit gently. Do not wash, peel or pit fruit. Only melon should be peeled, seeded and cut in large chunks. Layer fruit and sugar in prepared jar. Stir lightly. Pour rum over fruit to cover. Seal jar tightly.

Let mature in cool dark place 3 months. The Rumpot can be added to as more fruit becomes available. Always add equivalent sugar and more rum, if necessary, to keep fruit covered.

Serve with cream or yogurt, add to fresh fruit salad, or use to fill hollowed-out melon, or tart shell.

LIQUEURS

Liqueurs are a sweetened alcoholic beverage flavored with fruit or aromatics. Serve in liqueur glasses as an after dinner drink or use as a sauce for ice cream or other dessert. Use drained fruit as a dessert with cream.

Prepare fruit or fruit juice according to recipe. Add sugar and flavorings.

Cook fruit juice and sugar according to recipe. Ladle into prepared jar or bottle.

Fill jar or bottle with spirits, such as brandy, rum, gin or vodka. Cover tightly. Let mature for 3 to 12 weeks, according to recipe. Shake jar occasionally. Filter liqueur into clean bottle. Seal tightly.

Orange Shrub

2½ cups fresh orange juice, strained

4½ cups sugar

4½ cups light rum

Wash a ½ gallon jar and lid in hot soapy water; rinse. In a large saucepan, cook orange juice and sugar over low heat. Stir until sugar dissolves. Increase heat; boil 5 minutes, skimming off foam occasionally. Remove from heat; cool. Combine syrup and rum in prepared jar. Seal jar tightly. Let mature 2 weeks. Shake jar well each day. Let mature 4 weeks without disturbing. Filter liquid into 5 clean ½ pint bottles. Seal tightly.

Makes 5 (½ pints).

Cherry Brandy

1 lb. Morello cherries, pitted

2 whole cloves

½ cup sugar

Approximately 4 cups brandy

Wash a ½ gallon jar and lid in hot soapy water; rinse. Pack cherries into prepared jar. Add cloves, sugar and brandy. Seal jar tightly.

Let mature 12 weeks. Shake jar occasionally. Pour brandy into 4 clean 1 pint bottles. Seal tightly.

Makes 2 (1 pints).

Coffee Liqueur

1⅓ cups dark brown sugar

⅔ cup water

2 tablespoons instant coffee powder

2½ cups brandy

Wash a 1 quart jar and lid in hot soapy water; rinse. In a large saucepan, cook sugar and water over low heat 5 minutes. Skim off foam if necessary. Add coffee. Stir well; cool. Pour into prepared jar. Add brandy. Seal jar tightly.

Let mature 1 week. Shake bottle each day. Filter liquid into 2 clean 1 pint bottles. Seal tightly.

Makes 2 (1 pints).

SYRUPS

Syrups are a thick solution of fruit juice, sugar and water. They can be made from soft fruits or tangy citrus fruits. Use over pancakes, biscuits or waffles, dilute with water as a drink or serve as a sauce with dessert.

Use clean ripe fruit. Wipe fruit instead of washing. If required remove peel in long strips.

If required squeeze juice from fruit. In a large saucepan, cook fruit or juice over low heat. Crush fruit several times. Strain through a jelly bag 12 hours. In a large saucepan cook juice, sugar and water. Use 1½ cups sugar for each 2½ cups juice. Stir sugar until dissolved. Continue cooking according to recipe directions.

Pour into hot, sterilized bottles. Attach clean lids tightly. Place in canner. Release tops ½ turn. Process in a boiling water bath, page 13, 30 minutes. Remove bottles. Tighten tops immediately.

Blackcurrant Syrup

6 lb. blackcurrants, stems removed

2½ cups water

Sugar

Wash 5 (½ pint) bottles and lids in hot soapy water; rinse. Keep hot until needed.

In a large saucepan, simmer blackcurrants and water over low heat 1 hour. Crush blackcurrants several times. Strain through a jelly bag 12 hours. Measure juice. Measure 1½ cups sugar for each 2½ cups juice. In a saucepan stir sugar into juice over a low heat. Stir until sugar dissolves. Increase heat; bring to boil without stirring.

Strain hot syrup into 1 hot bottle at a time, leaving ½-inch headspace. Wipe rim of bottle with a clean damp cloth. Attach lid. Fill and close remaining bottles. Place in canner. Release lids ½ turn. Process in a boiling water bath, page 13, 30 minutes. Remove bottles. Tighten lids immediately.

Makes 5 (½ pints).

Raspberry Syrup

4 lb. raspberries

Sugar

Water

Place raspberries in a jelly bag. Squeeze to extract juice. Measure juice. Measure 2 cups sugar and 2½ cups water for each 2½ cups juice. In a large saucepan, cook sugar and water over low heat. Stir until sugar dissolves. Add juice. Increase heat; bring to boil. Reduce heat; simmer 1 hour. Remove from heat; cool completely.

Wash 5 (½ pint) bottles and lids in hot soapy water; rinse. Keep hot until needed.

Pour cold syrup into 1 hot bottle at a time, leaving ½-inch headspace. Wipe rim of bottle with a clean damp cloth. Attach lids. Fill and close remaining bottles. Place in canner. Release lids ½ turn. Process in a boiling water bath, page 13, 30 minutes. Remove bottles. Tighten lids immediately. Or, pour cold syrup into clean freezer containers leaving ½-inch headspace. Attach lid. Store in freezer up to 12 months.

Makes 5 (½ pints).

Orange Syrup

Peel of 6 Valencia oranges, cut in strips

4 cups sugar

4½ cups water

2½ cups fresh orange juice

2 tablespoons citric acid

In a large saucepan, cook orange peel strips, sugar and water over a low heat. Stir until sugar dissolves. Increase heat; boil 3 minutes. Remove from heat; cool. Strain through a jelly bag 12 hours. Add orange juice and citric acid. Mix well.

Wash 5 (1 pint) bottles and lids in hot soapy water; rinse. Keep hot until needed.

Pour hot syrup into 1 hot bottle at a time, leaving ½ inch headspace. Wipe rim of bottle with a clean damp cloth. Attach lids. Fill and close remaining bottles. Place in canner. Release lids ½ turn. Process in a boiling water bath, page 13, 30 minutes. Remove bottles. Tighten lids immediately.

Makes 5 (1 pints).

FLAVORED VINEGARS

Flavored vinegars may be added to salad dressings and mayonnaise or use in pickles and sauces. Mix vinegar in glass, enamel or stainless steel bowls. Store in glass bottles or jars with a cork or vinegar-proof tops.

Place herbs or other flavoring material in a sterilized jar.

Fill jar with wine vinegar or cider vinegar. Seal tightly. Let stand 2 weeks.

Strain through a jelly bag or cheesecloth. Add a little flavoring material, such as a sprig of tarragon, for an attractive appearance, if desired. Seal tightly.

Citron Vinegar

2 lemons

Grated peel of ½ orange

Grated peel and juice of 2 limes

---

4 ½ cups white wine vinegar

Pinch of salt

Pinch of paprika

Strips of lemon peel, to finish

Slice 1 lemon crosswise. Thread on a wooden skewer; grate peel of remaining lemon. In a large saucepan, bring skewer of lemons, lemon and orange peel, lime peel and juice, vinegar, salt and paprika to a boil. Remove from heat; cool completely. Transfer to a sterilized jar. Seal tightly with vinegar-proof lid. Let stand on a sunny or warm windowsill 2 weeks. Strain through a jelly bag.

Wash 5 (½ pint) jars or bottles and lids in hot soapy water; rinse. Sterilize in boiling water.

Place strips of lemon peel in prepared jars or bottles. Pour vinegar into jars or bottles. Wipe rim of jars or bottles with a clean damp cloth. Seal tightly with vinegar-proof lids.

Makes 5 (½ pints).

Raspberry Vinegar

2 lb. raspberries

5 cups red or white wine vinegar

Sugar

In a large bowl, cover raspberries with vinegar. Cover with a cloth. Let stand in a cool place 4 days. Strain through a jelly bag. Press fruit lightly. Measure juice. Measure ½ cup sugar for each 2½ cups juice. In a medium saucepan, cook juice and sugar over low heat, 15 minutes. Strain through a jelly bag.

Wash 5 (½ pint) jars or bottles and vinegar-proof lids in hot soapy water; rinse. Sterilize in boiling water.

Pour vinegar into prepared jars or bottles, leaving ½-inch head-space. Wipe rims of jars or bottles with a clean damp cloth. Seal tightly with vinegar-proof lids.

Makes 5 (½ pints).

Herb Vinegar

1 cup loosely packed fresh herbs, such as tarragon, basil, marjoram, thyme, fennel or mint

2 cups white wine vinegar

1 fresh herb sprig

Place herbs in a sterilized jar. Fill with vinegar. Seal tightly with vinegar-proof lid. Let stand 2 weeks. Strain through a jelly bag.

Wash 1 (1 pint) jar or bottle and a vinegar-proof lid in hot soapy water; rinse. Sterilize in boiling water.

Place a fresh herb sprig in prepared jar or bottle. Pour flavored vinegar into jar or bottle, leaving ½-inch headspace. Wipe rim of jar or bottle with a clean damp cloth. Seal tightly with a vinegar-proof lid.

Makes 1 (1 pint).

MUSTARDS

Mustard is a pungent condiment. Serve in small quantities with cheese, meats and poultry or add to sauces and salad dressings. Mustard can be prepared from crushed mustard seeds or mustard powder, see Aromatic Mustard Powder page 117.

Soak mustard seeds in lukewarm water 12 hours if a smooth result is required.

Crush seeds with a wooden spoon, in a mortar and pestle, in a food processor/blender or in a coffee grinder.

Mix crushed seeds with vinegar and chosen herbs, spices, salt and pepper as specified in recipe. Pack into sterilized jars. Seal tightly. Let mature several days before using.

Aromatic Mustard Powder

4 cups mustard powder

1 cup salt

1 tablespoon garlic powder

1 tablespoon dried thyme, crushed

1 tablespoon dried tarragon, crushed

1 tablespoon ground mixed spice

In a small bowl mix mustard powder and salt until evenly colored. Stir in garlic powder, thyme, tarragon and mixed spice. Spoon into sterilized jars. Seal tightly. To use, mix with water or vinegar, or add 1 to 2 pinches to soup and stews.

Makes 3 (½ pints).

Extra Strong Mustard

4 tablespoons white mustard seeds

½ teaspoon ground nutmeg

½ teaspoon grated horseradish

¼ teaspoon ground allspice

8 tablespoons white wine vinegar

Salt and pepper

In a food processor/blender or a coffee grinder, crush mustard seeds. In a small saucepan cook mustard seeds with nutmeg, horseradish, allspice and vinegar over low heat 5 minutes or until thick and creamy. Cool completely. Add salt and pepper to taste. Spoon into a sterilized jar. Seal tightly.

Let mature 1 week before using.

Makes 8 tablespoons.

Household Mustard

1¼ cups water

2 teaspoons sea salt

4 tablespoons white mustard seeds

8 tablespoons white wine vinegar

Salt and pepper

In a small saucepan, boil water and sea salt. Remove from heat. Let stand until lukewarm. In a medium bowl, pour salt water over mustard seeds. Let stand 12 hours: drain. Using a wooden spoon, crush seeds until soft and creamy.

In a small saucepan, bring vinegar to a boil. Gradually add to mustard. Add salt and pepper to taste. Spoon into a sterilized jar. Seal tightly.

Let mature several days before using. Will keep up to 1 month.

Makes 1 (½ pints).

CANDIED FRUITS

Candied fruit is a confection which may be eaten as a candy or used in cakes and desserts.

Do not hurry candying; it is important to allow the fruit to become saturated in the sugar syrup over several days, or the fruit will be tough and wrinkled.

Fruit should be fresh and of high quality without blemishes. Prepare fruit by halving or slicing. Prepare syrup by dissolving sugar in water over low heat. Allow 1¼ cups water to ¾ cup sugar for each 1lb fruit.

Simmer fruit in syrup. Let stand according to recipe. Repeat process for up to 7 days until fruit has absorbed all liquid.

Arrange fruit in a single layer; dry in a sunny or warm place 4 to 5 days, turning fruit occasionally until fruit is firm but not dry. Store in an airtight container.

Candied Chestnuts

2 lb. chestnuts, shells removed

2 lb. sugar

2½ cups water

1 vanilla bean

In a large saucepan, cover chestnuts with water. Bring to a boil; boil 8 minutes. Discard liquid. Drain. Using a kitchen towel, rub off brown inner skins. In a large saucepan, cook sugar, water and vanilla bean over low heat. Stir until sugar dissolves. Simmer 5 minutes. Add chestnuts. Increase heat; boil 10 minutes. Remove vanilla bean. Pour syrup and nuts into a large bowl. Let stand 12 hours. Return to pan. Boil 1 minute. Return to bowl. Let stand 24 hours. Repeat process 3 times until syrup has been absorbed.

Preheat oven to 150F (65C). Cover a wire rack with waxed or parchment paper. Place chestnuts on wire rack. Bake in preheated oven with oven door open 2 hours or until firm. Remove from oven; cool.

Store in a container lined with waxed paper. Will keep up to 2 weeks.

Makes 2 lb.

Candied Peel

Peel of 2 oranges

Peel of 2 lemons

1 cup sugar

In a large saucepan, cover peel with water. Cook over low heat 1½ hours. Add more water if necessary. Add sugar. Stir until sugar dissolves. Increase heat; bring to a boil. Remove from heat. Let stand 12 hours. Bring to a boil. Reduce heat; simmer 5 minutes. Remove from heat. Let stand 12 hours. Bring to a boil. Reduce heat; simmer until peel has absorbed nearly all of syrup. Drain peel.

Preheat oven to 150F (65C). Cover a wire rack with waxed paper. Place peel on wire rack. Spoon a small amount of surplus syrup into center of each piece of peel. Cover loosely with waxed paper. Bake in preheated oven with oven door open about 1 hour or until peel is firm and sugar crystallized. Remove from oven. Cool.

Store in an airtight container.

Candied Apricots

8 cups sugar

2½ cups water

4 lb. just-ripe apricots

Carefully skin at top of each apricot, squeeze out pits. In a large saucepan, cook sugar and water over low heat. Stir until sugar dissolves. Simmer 5 minutes. Add apricots. Increase heat; bring to a boil. Remove from heat. Let stand 1 hour. Bring to a boil again. Let stand 1 hour. Repeat process 3 times.

In a large bowl, let fruit and syrup stand 12 hours. In a large saucepan, boil fruit and syrup 1 minute. Drain fruit. Boil syrup; pour over fruit. Let stand 12 hours. Repeat process 2 times until apricots are saturated and syrup is absorbed.

Cover a wire rack with waxed or parchment paper. Dry apricots on wire rack. Turn fruit occasionally until firm.

When firm, store in an airtight container. Will keep up to 3 months.

Makes 4 lb.

DRYING

Drying fruits, vegetables and herbs produces a product which is relatively free from moisture. Add dried products to casseroles and stews or serve fruit as a dessert with cream. Dried herbs have a stronger flavor than fresh and should be used sparingly.

Use fresh ripe fruit or firm vegetables. If using apples and pears, drop into cold salted water. Use 1 tablespoon salt to every 4½ cups water to prevent discoloration. Vegetables do not need soaking. Slice if necessary.

Spread in a single layer on oven or wire racks.

Dry in a 120 to 150F (50 to 65C) oven. Leave oven door slightly open so that air circulates and carries away moisture. Fruit should be soft, leathery and uncolored. Vegetables should be crisp and firm. Let stand at room temperature 12 hours. Store in airtight containers. Will keep up to 1 year.

Dried Herbs

Mint, tarragon, thyme, sage, basil, marjoram

Preheat oven to 120 to 150F (50 to 65C). Divide herbs in small bunches. Spread on baking sheets in thin layers. Bake in preheated oven 45 minutes until crisp and dry. Remove from oven. Let stand 12 hours.

Remove stems; rub herbs lightly with hands to break up leaves. Store in airtight container in a cool dark place. Label carefully; dried herbs can look very similar. Use within 4 to 6 months.

Dried Onions or Leeks

Onions or Leeks, as available

Cover oven racks with muslin. Preheat oven to 150F (65C).

If using onions, peel and remove any soft parts. Slice thinly crosswise; place on oven racks. If using leeks, strip off outer leaves. Slice crosswise in rings or cut into narrow lengthwise strips. Place on oven racks.

Bake in preheated oven 1 hour or until firm and crisp. Rearrange pieces several times to dry evenly.

Remove from oven. Let stand 12 hours. Store in airtight container.

To use, soak 15 minutes in cold water.

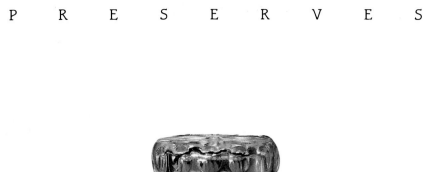

Dried Apple Rings

Firm, ripe apples, as available, peeled, cored.

Weak brine (2 tablespoons salt; 1¾ cups water)

Preheat oven to 150F (65C). Slice apples into 4-inch thick rings. In a large bowl, just cover apple rings with brine. Let stand 10 minutes. Drain apple rings; thread on wooden skewers.

Place skewers on oven shelves so apple rings do not touch. Bake in preheated oven 4 to 5 hours or until apple rings resemble soft leather and are moist and pliable.

Remove from oven. Let stand 12 hours. Store in airtight containers in a cool dry place.

To use, soak in fresh water 24 hours. In a medium saucepan, cook apples and liquid over low heat with a few strips of lemon peel, a vanilla bean or a pinch of ground cloves.

INDEX